PRAISE FOR *TEACHIN*
A LINGUISTICALLY AUᴛʜᴇɴᴛɪᴄ ꜰʀᴀᴍᴇᴡᴏʀᴋ
FOR EMERGING MULTILINGUALS

"Thankfully, the field of education is seeing a growing number of bilingual and dual-language programs. As we come to realize the critical need to grow the Spanish literacy of our multilingual learners, we must also equip our teachers with research-based, practical tools to do so. To meet this need, Rocio del Castillo-Perez and Julia Stearns Cloat have developed a user-friendly guide for teaching reading when the target language is Spanish. *Teaching Reading in Spanish: A Linguistically Authentic Framework for Emerging Multilinguals* is not only a practical guide, but it also offers readers much-needed reminders of equity, asset-based pedagogies, and culturally relevant practices."

—**Dr. Carol Salva**, educational consultant, Seidlitz Education

"In my twenty years working with multilinguals, I have never read such a comprehensive book about the art of teaching reading in Spanish. This book is easy to read and gives the reader all the tools necessary to improve literacy instruction for bilingual students. I love that the authors included key anchors that focused on asset-based pedagogies as well as seeing multilingualism from an additive perspective. I can't wait to use this as a book study with my staff!"

—**Dr. Maureen Cassidy**, executive director of English
learning, McHenry School District 15

"*Teaching Reading in Spanish* is a balance between theory, research, and application. With the rise in multilingual students in our districts, it's more important than ever to be responsive to their needs and teach literacy that is authentic to the language. This book weaves this knowledge throughout, creating a beautiful tapestry of how Spanish literacy works. The authors have also created a system for leveling books in Spanish—the DCC Leveling Instrument—a tool that is not yet out there in the field. This book is a must for districts that offer native language instruction in Spanish, as the information presented in this book will shift the thinking about linguistically and culturally appropriate instruction in Spanish."

—**Amy Mosquera**, principal consultant, Adelante
Educational Specialists Group

"In this book, del Castillo-Perez and Cloat offer an approachable framework for bilingual and dual language educators' Spanish literacy instruction that emphasizes knowing your students, implementing culturally and linguistically authentic literature, leveling books, and planning for meaningful instruction. In a time when educators are all-too-often deprofessionalized, *Teaching Reading in Spanish* extends the vast knowledge and professionalism required of bilingual and dual language educators by rooting its framework squarely in the legacy of civil rights movements (when bilingual education gained momentum nationwide) with their key anchors of equity, additive bilingualism, asset-based pedagogies, and culturally and linguistically relevant instructional practices. As someone who has been working in bilingual and dual-language settings for more than twenty-five years as a bilingual classroom teacher, literacy specialist, and professor, I can't wait for this book to be in the hands of bilingual and dual language educators. Their emerging multilingual students will benefit as a result."

—**Kimberley D. Kennedy, PhD**, founder and CEO, Pocket Profe

"Building on culturally relevant pedagogical tenets, insights, and practices, *Teaching Reading in Spanish* is one of its kind in truly highlighting multilingualism as an asset. Rocio del Castillo-Perez and Julia Stearns Cloat provide compelling research along with using their experiences as educators and district leaders, the foundation for not only the *what*, which is approaching biliteracy to teaching reading, but the *how* to integrate research into the daily reading block using content leveled texts and integrated biliteracy units. More important, the *why* behind their incredible work of love demonstrates how they are committed to providing better educational opportunities for all in a diverse world. This book is an example of how equity can be achieved through a linguistically authentic framework for our emerging multilingual learners—something that many districts have been working toward for many years."

—**Dr. Anna Alvarado**, superintendent of schools, Freeport School District

"The success of dual-language programs depends on the ability of classroom teachers to grow strong biliterate minds. This book answers so many questions that have been unanswered for years regarding Spanish bilingual reading instruction. It presents a holistic, comprehensive, and culturally appropriate biliteracy model for our U.S. classrooms. It also balances the theories of English instructional practices while considering Spanish linguistic nuances. It truly weaves a tapestry of our dual-language students, and I am so grateful del Castillo-Perez and Cloat have put forth this book to move our dual-language programs forward!"

—**Heather Robertson-Devine**, founder and CEO, Books del Sur

"*Teaching Reading in Spanish: A Linguistically Authentic Framework for Emerging Multilinguals* is a much needed and valuable resource for teachers of multilingual students in bilingual and dual-language classrooms. With a foundation in quality reading research and cultural responsiveness, DCC Lectura provides a system for assessing students, leveling books written in Spanish, and matching students to leveled books that will lead to high-quality reading instruction for emergent readers of Spanish. With easy-to-use resources, teachers can put DCC Lectura into action tomorrow!"

—**Tracy Mazurkiewicz**, multilingual reading specialist, Kaneland CUSD

"An untapped source of support that is often overlooked in biliteracy programs is the assets that students bring with them in their home language. This book makes a strong case for knowing, understanding, and leveraging those assets to support the biliteracy development of students who are native speakers of the partner language and those who are native speakers of English. Although there are many similarities in the English and Spanish languages, early literacy development in Spanish differs in many significant ways from English. This book highlights the similarities and expounds on the differences to allow teachers to better understand the importance of those differences as they seek to support their students' early literacy development in Spanish."

—**Kris Nicholls, PhD**, CEO, Nicholls Educational Consulting

"I cannot wait to put *Teaching Reading in Spanish: A Linguistically Authentic Framework for Emerging Multilinguals* in the hands of our dual-language teachers, psychologists, reading specialists, and administrators. This book is the next piece we have been looking for in reading instruction. It provides not only a framework for leveling text and the progress of students through the Spanish reading process but weaves in advocacy and culturally sustaining pedagogy. The DCC framework condenses all of the theory of reading instruction for emerging multilingual students into applicable practices. It integrates the complexity of culture, language, and reading acquisition into an authentic method for evaluating and instructing reading in multilingual classrooms. For too long, we have taught and assessed reading through 'Spanish a la English' due to not having a resource such as this. This also holds true in our MTSS practices. *Teaching Reading in Spanish* is just the resource we've been looking for to address the beautiful identities and learning practices of our emerging multilingual students."

—**AJ Crook**, bilingual programs coordinator, DeKalb
Community Unit School District 428

Teaching Reading in Spanish

A Linguistically Authentic Framework for Emerging Multilinguals

Rocio del Castillo-Perez
Julia Stearns Cloat

ROWMAN & LITTLEFIELD
Lanham • Boulder • New York • London

Published by Rowman & Littlefield
An imprint of The Rowman & Littlefield Publishing Group, Inc.
4501 Forbes Boulevard, Suite 200, Lanham, Maryland 20706
www.rowman.com

86-90 Paul Street, London EC2A 4NE, United Kingdom

British Library Cataloguing in Publication Information Available

Library of Congress Cataloging-in-Publication Data

Names: del Castillo-Perez, Rocio, 1971– author. | Cloat, Julia Stearns, 1968– author.
Title: Teaching reading in Spanish : a linguistically authentic framework for emerging
    multilinguals / Rocio del Castillo-Perez and Julia Stearns Cloat.
Description: Lanham : Rowman & Littlefield, [2022] | Includes bibliographical
    references and index. | Summary: "Teaching Reading in Spanish is an essential teacher
    instructional guide to developmental biliteracy. It provides a comprehensive reading
    framework for teachers who teach reading in K–12 dual language and bilingual
    programs"—Provided by publisher.
Identifiers: LCCN 2022027577 (print) | LCCN 2022027578 (ebook) | ISBN
    9781475864670 (cloth) | ISBN 9781475864687 (paperback) | ISBN
    9781475864694 (epub)
Subjects: LCSH: Spanish language—Study and teaching—English speakers | Spanish
    language—Study and teaching—Bilingual method. | Reading. | Education, Bilingual.
Classification: LCC PC4129.E5 C374 2022 (print) | LCC PC4129.E5 (ebook) | DDC
    468.4071—dc23/eng/20220822
LC record available at https://lccn.loc.gov/2022027577
LC ebook record available at https://lccn.loc.gov/2022027578

♾™ The paper used in this publication meets the minimum requirements of American
National Standard for Information Sciences—Permanence of Paper for Printed Library
Materials, ANSI/NISO Z39.48-1992.

Mi visión de la alfabetización va más allá del ba, be, bi, bo, bu. Porque implica una comprensión crítica de la realidad social, política y económica en la que está el alfabetizado. Enseñar exige respeto a los saberes y a la autonomía de los educandos, a saber escuchar.—Paulo Freire

Para mis tres amores. A Joel mi compañero de vida y a todos los que como él dejaron su tierra para seguir sus sueños. A Nicolas y a Bella, mis bilingües favoritos y con ellos, a todos los estudiantes bilingües, con el deseo de que siempre reconozcan el inmenso poder del bilingüismo.

Y para Julia, gracias mil por embarcarte en este proyecto conmigo, por ayudarme a entender y a "entenderme." Tu capacidad para "traducir" mis ideas y nuestro entorno no cesa de sorprenderme. Como el bilingüismo, juntas somos más fuertes.

No one is born fully formed: it is through self-experience in the world that we become what we are.—Paulo Freire
For Rocio, who has enriched my self-experience in ways that have fundamentally changed who I am. And for Max, who unconditionally supports every version of who I am.

Language is never neutral

—Paulo Freire

Contents

List of Tables

Foreword

Douglas Fisher

Reading is a gateway skill that provides access to the world of knowledge. Our students deserve the best possible instruction that allows them to read more and better every day. Over the past one hundred years, teachers have been honing their craft, based on published evidence, to ensure that students are taught to read. We have learned a great deal about the component parts of reading (e.g., phonemic awareness, phonics, fluency, vocabulary, and comprehension) and the value of teaching each of these aspects in a systemic, intentional way.

We are also clear that oral language development is critical in developing readers. As Britton (1983) noted, "Reading and writing float on a sea of talk" (p. 11). Further, "Oral comprehension sets the ceiling on reading comprehension" (Biemiller, 2003, n.p.). Thus, building oral language skills is a critical aspect of learning to read. Encouraging discussions about texts, the use of quality questions, and engaging students in listening comprehension tasks all contribute to reading development.

We also recognize that writing is the flip side of reading. Both develop in interrelated ways, and thus, writing should not be divorced from reading. Writing is the apex of language production and as such requires consolidation and coordination of multiple systems to encode, including composition, grammar, spelling, and idea generation (MacArthur et al., 2016).

I say this to note that the world has significant information and evidence about what it takes to ensure that students learn to read. Current estimates are that nearly 95% of students can be taught to read by the end of first grade (Moats, 2020). Unfortunately, nowhere near that number accomplish this level of performance. The sad truth is that some students do not receive the instruction necessary to ensure that they learn to read, and read well.

In some circles, the excuse for poor reading is the students' primary language. The logic seems to go this way: they can't learn to read well because they speak a language other than English at home. In reality, that is deficit thinking that limits the expectations educators have for students. We have sufficient knowledge to suggest that we can teach the vast majority of students to read, and read well.

Students can be taught to read in multiple languages and develop sophisticated code-switching skills, often referred to as translanguaging (Alfaro, 2020). This requires deep knowledge of both languages, including the print knowledge required for reading and writing. Educators of students learning to read in Spanish will find this book to be a powerful source of inspiration that will allow them to build their students' proficiency and serve as a scaffold to reading in both English and Spanish.

Dr. del Castillo-Perez and Dr. Cloat provide an instructional framework, based on sound linguistic practices, that can be used to design learning experiences for students. They provide a continuum of reading development, in Spanish, that allows teachers to identify instructional needs and take action to move students forward in their reading development. The authors note the ways in which educators can scaffold the learning experiences based on an individual student's current level of performance.

As part of their model, they describe leveling texts. This is not without controversy. The risk, as Alfred Tatum noted at the 2013 Michigan Reading Association conference, is that "leveled texts lead to leveled lives." Failing to continue to challenge students and keeping them in the same level of text for a long time does this damage. Failing to provide instructional scaffolds for increasingly complex texts does this damage. Failing to ensure that students practice and read widely does this damage.

But *Teaching Reading in Spanish* offers advice to counter these risks. The focus is on the instruction students need to read increasingly complex texts. And Dr. del Castillo-Perez and Dr. Cloat provide a clear path to proficiency. Teachers would be well-advised to learn the progressions outlined in the book and design amazing learning experiences that develop each skill so that students can access complex texts. Of course, teaching reading involves more than leveling texts, and students deserve direct and systematic instruction in each aspect of reading, writing, speaking, and listening. But the scaffolds that are outlined in this book, when done well, can ensure students' literacy learning.

REFERENCES

Alfaro, C. (2022, January 7). Code switching takes a lot of skill and a complex command of grammar. Retrieved from https://www.sandiegouniontribune.com/opinion/commentary/story/2022-01-07/opinion-code-switching-takes-a-lot-of-skill-and-a-complex-command-of-grammar

Biemiller, A. (2003, Spring). Oral comprehension sets the ceiling on reading comprehension. *American Educator* [Electronic edition]. Retrieved from: https://www.aft.org/periodical/american-educator/spring-2003/oral-comprehension-sets-ceiling-reading

Britton, J. (1983). Writing and the story of the world. In B. Kroll & E. Wells (Eds.), *Explorations in the development of writing theory, research, and practice* (pp. 3–30). New York: Wiley.

MacArthur, C., Graham, S., & Fitzgerald, J. (2016). *Handbook of writing research* (2nd ed.). New York: Guilford.

Moats, L. C. (2020). Teaching reading is rocket science. Retrieved from https://www.aft.org/ae/summer2020/moats

Preface

Once social change begins, it cannot be reversed. You cannot uneducate the person who has learned to read. You cannot humiliate the person who feels pride. You cannot oppress the people who are not afraid anymore.

—Cesar Chavez

Teaching Reading in Spanish: A Linguistically Authentic Progression for Emerging Multilinguals was written to be a practical resource for those who teach reading in dual-language and bilingual classrooms. It was built off of our experience working with and as teachers. *Teaching Reading in Spanish* was written with one goal in mind: to provide teachers with a comprehensive Spanish reading framework based on linguistically authentic pedagogy, not on English-language practices.

Parker Palmer said, "teaching holds a mirror to the soul," and a significant part of writing this book was the process of reflecting on our identities and our integrities. Before we could address technique, we had to pinpoint the key anchors to our work:

1. equity
2. additive multilingualism
3. asset-based pedagogies
4. culturally and linguistically relevant instructional practices and methods

The four key anchors are woven throughout the book and are more than a theoretical framework: they are principles for instruction that create environments for success.

We both currently work in preK–12 public-school districts and teach at the university level, where we are asked by teachers about the best way to teach multilingual learners. Teachers want to know which resources they should be using, how to teach phonics, about oracy, and translanguaging. We wrote this book for them and for you.

We have taken our more than fifty years of combined experience in literacy and biliteracy to create what we call the DCC lectura method. DCC connects our names together (del Castillo & Cloat) and represents the cross-linguistic connections between Spanish and English taught in dual-language and bilingual classrooms. The DCC lectura method applies a systematic literacy approach to biliteracy by weaving together a tapestry of relevant instructional components including phonemic and phonological awareness, oracy, decoding, fluency, background knowledge, vocabulary, language structures, verbal reasoning, and literacy knowledge.

Readers will find important guidance on topics relevant to working with emerging multilingual students, including using translanguaging as a relevant instructional tool, explicitly facilitating cross-linguistic connections, and providing students access to rich, diverse, and culturally relevant texts. The content and tools provided in this book and on our website, www.readingtapestry .com, are designed to provide teachers with a better understanding of how emerging multilingual students learn and to reflect the value of biliteracy, additive multilingualism, and multiculturalism.

HOW TO READ THIS BOOK

Teaching Reading in Spanish was written as a guide for teachers. We understand that the chapters may not be read in order or in their entirety. To make it as user friendly and simple to use as possible, we are providing a brief overview of each of the six chapters and how they all fit together.

Chapter 1: Introduction

Chapter 1 introduces the four key anchors of the work of DCC lectura. The goal for this chapter is to provide insight into our principles and who we are as teachers, as well as why we feel the approach provided in this book will benefit you and your students.

Chapter 2: The Science of Reading for Emergent Multilingual Learners

Chapter 2 begins with an overview of reading research as a way to create a foundation for building authentic and successful literacy experiences in dual-language and bilingual classrooms. In this chapter, we provide a comparative analysis of the foundation skills in Spanish and English so teachers are able to facilitate cross-linguistic connections.

We also introduce the Spanish Reading Tapestry as a cognitive framework for critical components of reading skills in Spanish. In this chapter we answer the most common questions that dual-language and bilingual teachers ask, including, "How do we teach students to read Spanish?" and introduce the DCC lectura method for teaching reading.

Chapter 3: Stages of Reader Development

Chapter 3 provides detailed descriptions of the seven stages of reader development as a structure for getting to know your students as readers and setting your instructional intentions. Practical tools such as the student interest inventory, family knowledge inventory, and the formative assessment of reader characteristics described in this chapter will help teachers build relationships with their students and determine the stage of reader development.

Chapter 4: Leveling Text

Chapter 4 first establishes the crucial distinction between students' stages of reader development and levels of text, then provides a practical guide to leveling authentic books. Using DCC lectura's leveling instrument, teachers will be able to level books that are already in their classrooms.

Chapter 5: Examples of Leveled Text

Chapter 5 provides exemplars of authentic Spanish texts that have been leveled using DCC lectura's leveling instrument and tables of text characteristics for each of the 21 levels. The pivotal characteristics at a given level are identified. Knowing these characteristics is helpful during the process of leveling books, while setting goals with students, and when prioritizing teaching points for small-group instruction.

Chapter 6: Leveled Books in the Classroom

Chapter 6 provides teachers specific tips for implementing leveled books in their classrooms. The chapter provides guidance for matching readers with appropriate leveled text, considerations for determining the instructional purpose, and the process for deciding which skills to teach and which instructional methods to use to teach them.

ACKNOWLEDGMENTS

The art of weaving is a profound metaphor for understanding the workings of the universe and our place in it. Through the physical process of weaving, we gain a better understanding of this world and how we as human beings are woven into it.

—Merrill, 2016

As our project has evolved, weaving has become a strong metaphor for our work. Through the process of grappling with concepts, research, and practices, we have woven together a tapestry of understandings. Dual-language and biliteracy teachers and advocates are a supportive and welcoming community, and through the process of compiling the work of experts for the appendixes, we experienced the unexpected joy of being enriched by this community of educators, researchers, and experts.

We are thankful for all of the gracious people who have discussed their ideas and experiences with us and were patient enough to answer our questions and help us to explore and expand our thinking. Alone, our individual threads of understanding would be loose strands, but when woven together with the collaboration of others, beautiful patterns emerged. The textile that is this book has been made more vibrant by everyone who has contributed to it, and we would like to thank each of them:

- Geri Chaffee: Thank you for your passion. The education system in the United States needs fierce advocates for dual language like you.
- Dr. Kris Nicholls: Thank you for sharing the importance of additive multilingualism. We truly appreciate your systematic approach to implementing dual-language classrooms.
- Heather Robertson-Devine: Thank you for your warmth, your friendship, and your knowledge of books.
- Amy Mosquera: Thank you for your deep understanding of the working of the dual-language classroom and how to best use paired text.
- Dr. Kim Kennedy: Thank you for being so very gracious and sharing your approach to teaching accents.

MAJOR CONTRIBUTIONS

Much of the foundation of this book is possible because of the work of those who have made major contributions to our research, either through their work in equity, literacy, biliteracy, or culturally sustaining teaching. We can't possibly thank all of the scholars, experts, and practitioners who have sat with us, whose research we have pored over, or the generous teachers who have opened their classrooms to us. Nor can we thank the countless friends and family members who have encouraged us in moments of doubt and the colleagues who have validated our ideas and the need to persevere in the writing of this book.

CALL TO ACTION

Sometimes advocacy is loud and demanding. Sometimes it is silent and powerful. It burns deeply in the heart of an educator who sees a child judged by a standard that discounts her very being.

—National Education Association

Working as and with teachers of multilingual students, we understand the importance of advocating for students and programs. It is likely that administrators, colleagues, and parents do not fully understand the intricacies of dual and bilingual instruction. Together, as educators who value equity and additive multilingualism, our moral imperative is to help administrators and fellow teachers understand and value the benefits of multilingualism.

Multilingualism should be promoted as a strength in education. Emergent multilinguals, like all students, enrich our school with their cultural traditions and language. This, together with their families' dreams, shapes our communities. Our current policies and practices characterize immigrants as linguistically deficient, but in truth these communities have always had their own stories to tell: stories of love, strength, resilience, and learning.

Advocacy bears many meanings for different individuals, but at its foundation, advocacy is about action. Sometimes advocating is as simple and effective as providing our students and families the means to advocate on their own behalf. Sometimes it means to learn everything possible about the laws and regulations governing multilingual students in your state. Sometimes it's creating strong connections with coworkers and community members, or extending beyond your area to pursue professional networks and development. Sometimes it's a ripple effect as the effort of one individual or small group motivates others to act.

As an advocate, you support your students by speaking up about what students want, what they need, and what their rights are. This is especially crucial for students from marginalized populations who may be less willing to stand up for themselves.

In addition to becoming a voice for your students, you serve to inform their families. You can assist students in understanding their rights at school and in the community. You can form connections with other groups and organizations to ensure that students can receive the resources they need. In general, you're a bridge between students and the world beyond the classroom, and you fill the gap between students' needs and the resources that may help them achieve. These are some questions that can guide your advocacy efforts:

- What can I do in my classroom?
- What can I do in my school?
- What can I do in my district?
- How can I support the families of my students?
- What can I do in my community?

Regardless of whether your advocacy is loud and demanding, or silent and powerful, we call to you to begin the social change that cannot be reversed.

Chapter 1

Introduction

Education is an act of love, and thus an act of courage.

—Paulo Freire

KEY POINTS IN CHAPTER 1

- *Emerging multilingual learner* is a term used to describe students who are in the process of becoming proficient in their home language(s) while learning to function in a new, additional language(s).
- Teachers and administrators must work to establish a culture of equity in which all students has access to the educational resources and rigor they need at the right moment in their education.
- Students learning Spanish in the United States will use their emerging knowledge of language as they develop their multiliteracy skills.
- The purpose of leveling text is to have appropriate materials to use during small-group instruction. The intention is never to level the students.

Teaching is an act of love and an act of courage. As teachers, our practices are rooted in our beliefs, and our beliefs are based on experience. We are called upon to engage in self-reflection so we can share ourselves with our students. As authors, we had a similar experience throughout the process of writing this book. We found ourselves reflecting on our beliefs and values so we could build an approach to teaching reading in Spanish that was rooted in our beliefs and was based on our experiences.

It is critical to us that before discussing the practical and specific aspects of teaching Spanish literacy and how our approach will benefit you and your students, we must first give insight into our principles and the beliefs that anchor the foundation of our practice.

KEY ANCHORS

In this chapter we look at the four key beliefs that anchor the DCC lectura approach to multiliteracy instruction and provide working definitions of the concepts and their implications in the classroom. This set of guiding principles and fundamental beliefs informs our work and guides our practices.

1. equity
2. additive multilingualism
3. asset-based pedagogies
4. culturally and linguistically relevant instructional practices and methods

Anchor 1: Equity

First and foremost, the approach taken in this book is rooted in equity. As educators, we must acknowledge the institutional inequities that exist, learn about them, and advocate for change to happen. According to the Equity Literacy Institute (2021), equity is about more than just providing all students with the resources they need to achieve success on an individual level. Thinking about fairness as equal distracts us from our responsibilities to overcome institutional bias and inequity in our society.

Instead, equity is a process by which we guarantee that policies, practices, institutional cultures, and ideologies are actively equitable and focused on the students and families whose interests we have not adequately addressed. In the short term, recognition and understanding of these types of inequities prepare us to react to them in an effective and timely manner. In addition, we improve our ability to effect long-term change by addressing the institutional and social factors that contribute to the occurrence of daily inequity.

As teachers, equity extends beyond how we treat students. In truth, an essential contrast is between treating your students equally and treating them equitably.

- Treating students equally means that all students receive the same treatment regardless of their needs.
- Treating students equitably means that all students receive what they need, when they need it.

Treating students *equally* can only be *equitable* if all students begin at the same starting point and can achieve success with the exact same opportunities, access, and resources. It is extremely unlikely that within one classroom, all students will be at the same starting point. Teachers and administrators must work to establish a culture of equity in which all students have access to the educational resources and rigor they need at the right moment in their education regardless of race, gender, ethnicity, language, disability, sexual orientation, family background, and/or family income.

It is our mission to help teachers build culturally sustaining teaching on a foundation of educational equity. Through the resources and information shared in this book, we strive to provide teachers and their students with resources and practices that are equitable to those available in English.

In truth, we must keep in mind that equity is a foundation, mind-set, and approach. But teachers can take steps to make the learning environment and the instruction more inclusive. These ideals are woven throughout the book and are summarized here:

1. Acknowledge Your Biases

As teachers, we frequently think that we can be objective with our students. Despite our best efforts, we all have values, beliefs, and predispositions that influence how we interact with others. These assumptions aren't always bad because they might help us grasp unfamiliar circumstances or make sense of what's going on around us. However, when our preconceptions materialize as implicit biases that might lead to forced identities, we unconsciously perpetuate unfavorable stereotypes and school cultures (Hanselman et al., 2014).

In reality, teachers' implicit biases may frequently lead to lowered goals or expectations for children of color and from underserved communities. Understanding hidden associations, assumptions, or biases allows us to gain a better understanding of our "self" so we can collaborate with "others" to achieve a mediated identity in which positive academic and social identities can be affirmed and nurtured (Delpit, 1995; Nieto & Bode, 2011).

2. Get to Know Your Students

Understanding who your students are and their interests can assist you in providing them with high-quality learning opportunities. Getting to know students and the factors that influence their personal and family lives will help teachers make lessons more culturally sustaining and build relationships. Considering factors such as socioeconomic status, family makeup, the educational expectations, and goals they have for the child will provide opportunities to make the learning experiences more personalized and better meet the students' needs.

3. Differentiate Your Teaching and Curriculum

To embrace culturally sustainable practices in your classroom, consider what you have learned about your students and make sure that your focus, standards, instructional approaches, and materials reflect their cultures and expose them to different cultures. In addition, authentic forms of assessment tools (e.g., observations, rubrics, conferring, performance tasks) are a more culturally and linguistically sustaining way to assess student performance and progress than more traditional classroom assessments.

4. Involve Family and Community

Making the learning environment in your classroom more inclusive and culturally sustaining means engaging families and communities in the school lives of students. By supporting students' bicultural and multicultural identity development, families will feel more included and more comfortable, ultimately, making it more likely that they become partners with their children's school.

Anchor 2: Asset-Based Pedagogies

Asset-based pedagogies are a counter to deficit-based paradigms of education. An asset-based approach to education is crucial in attaining equity in our classrooms. Teachers and students are respected for what they provide to the classroom rather than being characterized by what they may lack or need to improve. In an asset-based approach, every community is valued; every community has strengths and potential. Asset-based pedagogies seek to unleash students' potential by concentrating on their abilities and talents.

An asset-based approach to teaching focuses on what students *can* do rather than what they *cannot* do. Switching from deficits to assets when addressing marginalized students embodies a growth mind-set. In an asset-based pedagogy, everyone has assets from which the classroom community builds knowledge collectively. In this learning environment teachers constantly ask themselves, *What is present that I can build upon?*

Teachers strive to understand who their students are and how they might be missing from the curriculum. Ensuring equity for all students relies on teachers viewing student differences as assets and not deficits while having high expectations for all. Asset-based teaching does not perpetuate deficit perspectives and consciously acknowledges students as a resource that provides intellectual capital and contributions to teaching and learning (Civil, 2017).

The most recent educational philosophy, culturally sustaining pedagogy (CSP), builds, affirms, and respects the key components of the asset-based pedagogies, such as culturally responsive practices (CRP) that preceded it, and improves upon them by putting the students' cultures at the center of learning. The goal is for students to retain their cultural and linguistic roots (Gay, 2000; Moll & Gonzalez, 2009; Paris & Alim, 2017). Ladson-Billings's CRP (1995) serves as the foundation of this new approach.

The evolution from CRP to CSP reflects the needs of our changing educational systems and our increasingly diverse student population. Rather than eradicate the cultures of students, educators must help students sustain, embrace, and validate their cultures by connecting present learning to the histories of communities, neighborhoods, cities, and nation-states. As Paris and Alim (2017) assert, "it is crucial when we are seeking to sustain valuable practices that we link those practices up with the past and present of communities." To infuse CSP into classrooms, take an additive approach to the language, literacy, and ways of being of students.

As teachers, we shouldn't treat aspects of culture as marginal or simply to be added to the existing curriculum. Rather, facets of students' selves and communities must be centered meaningfully in classroom learning, across units and projects. The type of institutionalized change needed for this mind shift cannot occur through a single initiative or concrete practice, but teachers are in a position to ignite transformation and be their students' advocate.

Anchor 3: Additive Multilingualism

The number of students in U.S. public schools who speak a language other than English at home is on the rise, and classrooms are becoming increasingly multilingual. In the United States, students have daily opportunities to hear and use both their home language(s) and English (Grosjean, 2016).

As students are in continuous contact with multiple languages, they develop skills in their home language while learning to function in English and are considered to be emergent multilingual. *Emerging multilingual learner* is a term used to describe students who are in the process of becoming proficient in their home language(s) while learning to function in a new, additional language(s).

While emerging bilingual and emerging multilingual are both terms that reflect the additive nature of learning more than one language, emerging multilingual is primarily used in this book. We believe emerging multilingual to be a more inclusive term that reflects the linguistic repertoire of all students who are learning to function in two or more languages. To learn more about additive multilingualism, read "Additive Approach to Multilingualism" by Dr. Kris Nicholls in appendix B.

Emergent multilingual learners draw on different language systems. The linguistic repertoire of emerging multilingual students taps into all languages available to them as they learn to read and write. Through a process called translanguaging, bilinguals access different linguistic features or various modes of what are described as autonomous languages to maximize communicative potential (García, 2009).

To be clear, translanguaging is not code switching. Code switching is based on the assumption that the two or more languages of multilinguals are distinct monolingual codes that may be used independently and without reference to each other.

Research in neurolinguistics has proven that multilinguals do not have distinct languages; rather, they have one linguistic repertoire that contains elements of all the languages they speak. Bilinguals are not merely two monolinguals combined into a single individual; instead, it is more accurate to say that they are individuals whose language incorporates features of all of the languages they speak (Grosjean, 1989).

Translanguaging holds that bilinguals have a single language repertoire from which they strategically select elements in order to communicate successfully. Effective multilingual education entails the use of techniques to draw on all of the linguistic resources that every student has, as well as the development of methods to assist students in drawing on all of their linguistic resources (Grosjean, 2010; Bialystok, 2011).

Anchor 4: Relevant Instructional Methods and Authentic Materials

Researchers have shown the many benefits of providing students access to culturally relevant and authentic books and materials (Dixson & Fasching-Varner, 2009; Gay, 2000, 2002; Ladson-Billings, 1994). The books selected to be used with emerging multilingual students should be culturally sustaining, authentically representing, and validating of the students' cultures. Having access to and reading high-quality books about people of their own culture can engage students' emotions and encourage them to find literature that is meaningful to them.

Further, research has shown that reading comprehension of emerging multilingual students improves when they are exposed to culturally relevant books (Harris, 1997; McNair, 2010). As teachers and advocates of dual-language and bilingual programs, we should take care to intentionally select authentic texts, written originally in Spanish, and to carefully consider when translations may be appropriate. Heather Robertson-Devine has contributed a piece on Spanish book collections (see appendix C) that addresses the three categories of books that are found in dual-language and bilingual classrooms.

Spanish Versus English Leveled Text

Leveled text is a key component of a framework for literacy instruction that balances whole-group and small-group learning experiences. Through an explicit and systematic approach to teaching reading and writing, leveled text is used during all aspects of literacy instruction—aligning the text level or stage of reader development to the instructional purpose.

Experts in biliteracy instruction (Beeman & Urow, 2013; Escamilla, 2001; Potowski, 2010; Valdes, 2011) stress the importance of explicitly pointing out the similarities and differences between Spanish and English during literacy instruction in U.S. classrooms. As Beeman & Urow point out, "Students learning Spanish in the US will develop their language differently than students in Spanish-speaking countries" (p. 10) and will use their emerging knowledge of language as they develop their multiliteracy skills.

For this reason, it is important for teachers to understand the similarities and differences between English and Spanish to provide a more coherent literacy environment for students. Later in *Teaching Reading in Spanish: A Linguistically Authentic Framework for Emerging Multilinguals*, we will look at the similarities and differences between key features of English and Spanish and provide suggestions for instruction.

Introduction to DCC Lectura Leveling Instrument

The DCC lectura leveling instrument was created to provide teachers with a way to use authentic Spanish books for systematic reading instruction. It allows teachers to efficiently and accurately determine the levels of Spanish text. It is comparable to other systems in English in that it provides teachers with the text levels to be used for small-group instruction. However, DCC lectura's leveling instrument has the added benefits of being standards-based and aligned with seven distinct stages of reader development.

The stages of reader development designed by DCC lectura provides teachers with a research-based framework for thinking about students' reading behaviors in a way that is respectful of each student's own biliteracy journey while still maintaining the rigor of grade-level standards. Teachers simply identify the reader characteristics that they have observed in their students to determine the students' stages of reader development.

DCC lectura's leveling instrument is based on the Spanish version of the Common Core State Standards (2010) and the Texas Essential Knowledge and

Skills (TEKS, 2017). The leveling instrument includes detailed descriptions of text based on three basic systems: surface, linguistic and meaning-making (Keene, 2006). The systems, described in detail in chapter 3, include characteristics of text that together create a detailed and comprehensive structure for the leveling of Spanish books.

Leveling for Your Students, Not of Your Students

According to a study conducted by the National Governors Association Center for Best Practices (2010), when teaching reading it is not enough to ask high-order questions and to teach comprehension strategies. Teachers must also challenge students to read increasingly complex text. Using leveled books has been proven to be a highly effective instructional tool that helps to systematize the process of instructing students with increasingly complex text.

It is vital to keep in mind that the purpose of leveling text is to have appropriate materials to use during small-group instruction. The intention is *never* to level the students, but to match students' current stage of reader development with the level of text that appropriately challenges them during small-group instruction.

As many have asserted (Fountas & Pinnell, 2019; Serravallo, 2018), levels were never intended to be a child's label or identity. Matching leveled text with readers is not an exact science. The student's background knowledge, vocabulary, and interests will influence the level of text that is appropriate for instruction (Richardson, 2016). Students often will have more than one level of text that is a good match for their current reading abilities, and the exact level will have to be determined by the instructional purpose.

Overview of Instructional Practices

Chapters 2 and 6 provide details about instructional structures and strategies, but we believe it would be beneficial to have an overview of the instructional practices in mind throughout this book to better imagine how all systems, structures, and strategies fit together.

Fisher and Frey (2008) determined that four basic instructional moves promote learning: focus lesson, guided instruction, collaborative work, and independent work. Basic instructional design includes a systematic gradual release of responsibility beginning with the teacher providing direct instruction and modeling during a focus lesson for the whole group.

Then the teacher establishes a series of learning opportunities for the students that intentionally promote independence by lessening the support that teachers and peers provide to the student. The following bullet points show the alignment of the stage of gradual release, the instructional structures in the reading block, and the DCC lectura system that will guide text selection for instruction.

Instructional Structure	System to Guide Text Selection
• Whole Group: Focus Lesson	• Stage Reader Development
• Small Group: Strategy-Skill Group	• Leveling/Stage of Reader Development
• Small Group: Guided Reading	• Leveling Instrument
• Collaborative Literacy Tasks	• Leveling/Stage of Reader Development
• Individual: Conferring	• Leveling Instrument
• Individual: Independent Reading	• Stage of Reader Development

When planning instructional structures that are broader in scope (i.e., whole-group and collaborative tasks) or purpose (i.e., independent reading), it is appropriate to select books within the entire range of the stage of reader development. When planning instructional structures designed for *specific skills* (i.e., guided reading, strategy-skill group) or for individual students (i.e., conferring), it is best to select books at a specific level that are a good match for the student(s).

Chapter 2

The Science of Reading for Emergent Multilingual Learners

Good teaching cannot be reduced to technique; good teaching comes from the identity and integrity of the teacher.

—Parker Palmer

KEY POINTS IN CHAPTER 2

- The first step to teaching reading through an asset-based pedagogy mind-set is to embrace the additive nature of multilingualism.
- The multilingual classroom in which Spanish and English are taught contains three linguistic spaces: Spanish, English, and the cross-linguistic space where connections between both languages are facilitated by the teacher.
- Providing opportunities for students to engage in oral language will promote language development, which is especially important for multilingual learners.
- Teachers who understand the similarities and differences between Spanish and English will be able to provide more authentic and successful literacy experiences for their students and facilitate the cross-linguistic connections between languages.

The first step in taking an asset-based approach to instruction in a dual-language or bilingual classroom is to embrace the additive nature of multilingualism. Teachers who understand the similarities and differences between Spanish and English will be able to provide authentic and successful literacy experiences for their students and facilitate the cross-linguistic connections between languages.

The goal of chapter 2 is to use the body of research referred to as the science of reading (SoR). This chapter will also take a close look at the aspects of reading that are universal to English and Spanish and to those that are specific to Spanish and will need to be taught through an explicit, systematic approach. It will do this by providing an overview of summaries of the SoR in English and how it can be adapted successfully to teach reading in Spanish. Simply put, our goal is to equip teachers with specific information and strategies so they are better able to teach scaffolded Spanish reading skills in an authentic way.

The Science of Reading: What Is It?

In essence, the science of reading (SoR) is a term commonly used to refer to a body of research comprising decades of scientific knowledge that spans many languages and fields including education, psychology, neurology, and literacy (Ordetx, 2021). SoR has had a direct influence on how teachers of reading understand the complexities of learning to read, the cognitive systems involved, and the intricate skills that need to be taught explicitly—and what happens if those skills are *not* taught in an explicit, systematic manner.

In fact, SoR has managed to debunk various instructional methods that were not based on scientific evidence but had still been commonly used to teach reading. The result of this intersection of science and education translates into evidence-based practices for teaching foundational literacy skills called structured literacy.

Structured Literacy: What Are the Instructional Implications of SoR?

Structured literacy is an overarching term that the International Dyslexia Association (2018) coined to describe evidence-based approaches and strategies to teach reading. A structured literacy approach is based on how a child's brain acquires and processes information and explicitly teaches systematic word identification and decoding strategies. The skills build upon one another systematically and cover the following concepts: phonology, orthography (sound-symbol relationships), syllables, morphology, syntax, and semantics.

The organization of material follows the logical order of the language, beginning with the easiest and most basic concepts and elements and progressing methodically to more difficult concepts and elements. All students benefit from structured literacy, but this is especially true of students who are emerging bilingual, low-income, and students with dyslexia. Structured literacy's explicit approach to teaching reading provides teachers with a way to tailor teaching and instruction to learners who need it most.

It has been said that reading is the most complex thing that people are ever taught how to do. Teachers rely on research to ensure that they use the most effective methods with their students, but the long-standing controversy over the role of phonics in reading instruction complicates knowing what to believe (Kim, 2008).

Two common reading frameworks help teachers to better understand the comprehensive body of SoR research that supports a structured literacy approach: the simple view of reading and Scarborough's reading rope. Much has been written and discussed about each of these frameworks, so the scope of this book will focus on understanding their implications on teaching students to read Spanish.

Simple View of Reading

Comprehension is always the ultimate goal for reading instruction, and reading comprehension is driven by two broad skill sets that are identified in the simple view of reading. The simple view of reading is a formula that depicts the widely understood concept that reading has two basic components: word recognition (decoding) and language comprehension. Gough and Tunmer (1986) presented a formula that depicts the essence of reading. It shows that a student's reading comprehension (RC) can be predicted based on the students decoding skills (D) and language comprehension (LC).

- Decoding (D) x Language Comprehension (LC) = Reading Comprehension (RC)

In the simple view formula, the two basic components of reading are multiplied and not added, meaning that if a child has either zero decoding skills or zero language comprehension, the resulting comprehension will *also* be zero. Skillful reading depends on both decoding skills and language comprehension. The purpose of this research-based formula is to clarify that decoding is essential to successful reading.

Widely spread past and current practice have led teachers to believe that if students have strong background knowledge, vocabulary, and language comprehension, they will be able to comprehend what they are reading. Common "top-down" approaches to reading instruction led teachers to believe that strong decoding skills were unnecessary and encouraged students to rely on strategies such as using picture clues, skipping words, using sentence structure, guessing the word based on the first sound, and asking themselves if the sentence makes sense.

Taking a top-down approach is problematic to beginning and struggling readers of both Spanish and English. In contrast, the simple view of reading stresses the importance of explicitly teaching students to decode unfamiliar words using all of the letters in the word and to practice reading accurately until automaticity is achieved.

Scarborough's Reading Rope

The simple view of reading looks at reading through a wide-angle lens, only looking at the broadest components of reading instruction. In contrast, Scarborough's reading rope zooms into the components of reading instruction to consider all of the subskills included in the two essential components of the simple view of reading. Scarborough's reading rope was first introduced by Dr. Hollis Scarborough as a way to explain to parents the complex nature of reading and how the strands of reading weave together with shared interconnectedness and interdependence (International Dyslexia Association, 2018).

Scarborough's reading rope takes an extremely complex process and shows the importance of each component and how they are woven together to create the strong, successful reading of English. Using this uncomplicated metaphor helps to explain that if any strand or thread is frayed, the resulting rope of reading will be weaker.

For teachers in dual-language and biliteracy classrooms, the challenge of Scarborough's reading rope is that it is a model built to explain to parents the complexities of learning to read *English*. Because the simple view of reading has a broader view of reading, it is universal to any language. In contrast, certain threads of the reading rope are language specific. In the next section of this chapter the commonalities and differences between English and Spanish are broken down and reconstructed as a literacy framework that applies SoR to teaching reading in Spanish.

A BILITERACY APPROACH TO TEACHING READING

Reading and language are inextricably tied together. To be successful, teachers of multilingual students must understand the similarities and differences between Spanish and English to provide more authentic and successful literacy experiences for students.

Taking a meta-linguistic approach will help students recognize the relationships between Spanish and English and set them up to achieve higher levels of language proficiency, potentially allowing for greater academic achievement than students who regard their languages as distinct and unconnected (Beeman & Urow, 2013). Given program models or curricula may separate the languages of instruction, but the biliterate brain will continue to seek connections, providing teachable moments for dual-language and bilingual teachers.

In dual and biliteracy classrooms in the United States, teachers of emerging multilingual learners may want to consider the literacy skills and concepts that are universal and those that are language specific. Universal skills and concepts must be learned by all students who are learning to read, regardless of the language.

Some universal skills, such as the alphabetic principle, will be learned by most students through exposure and in the context of the learning environment. Other universal skills and concepts will need to be taught explicitly in one language; but because they are transferable across languages, they will not need to be taught explicitly in both languages. In contrast, skills and concepts that are language specific must be taught explicitly to all emerging multilinguals (Odlin, 1989; Center for Applied Linguistics, 2016; Ford & Palacios, 2015).

Table 2.1 includes specific concepts that are universal and transfer across all languages and those that are language specific.

The primary differences between teaching students to read Spanish and teaching them to read English occur during the early reading stages. This is due to the differences between the English and Spanish orthographies (spelling systems). Although Spanish and English both have orthographic systems that map sounds to the print on the page, each language has its own system of letter/sound relationships.

Although English has only 26 letters, the letters, or a combination of letters, can produce 44 possible phonemes. Students learning to read English must learn strategies to manipulate phonemes by segmenting, blending, deleting, and so forth. In contrast, Spanish has 27 letters but only 22–24 phonemes, thereby making Spanish a very phonetically consistent language.

It is commonly understood by teachers who have taught children to read English text that students learning to read English will typically spend three to four years developing reading skills until they can read fluently. In

Table 2.1

	Universal Concepts
Alphabetic Principle	Early readers of alphabetic languages (e.g., English and Spanish) learn that marks on pages are symbols that represent sounds.
Orthographic Awareness	Early in reading development, students will understand that letters combine to form words, phrases, and sentences. Bilingual students are able to apply the spelling system that they learn in one language within and across languages (Guilamo, 2021).
Meaningfulness of Print	A powerful source of transfer across languages is the concept that print carries meaning. Readers know that reading is about deriving meaning from print. Using comprehension strategies to make meaning is a skill that transfers across languages.
Identity as a Reader/ Writer	Students who see themselves as readers and writers in one language will be able to transfer these beliefs and attitudes about interacting with text to other languages.
Higher-Level Thinking	Conceptual understanding and metacognitive strategies (e.g., predicting, questioning, inferring, determining central idea) transfer across languages.
Content Knowledge	This is an especially important concept in dual-language classrooms. Knowledge and concepts acquired in one language do not need to be retaught in a second language. Knowledge transfers across languages.
	Language-Specific Concepts
Grammar	Each language has its own grammar rules.
Orthographic Features	Although Spanish and English both have orthographic systems that map sounds to the print on the page, each language has its own system of letter/sound relationships. Although English has only 26 letters, the letters or a combination of letters can produce 44 possible phonemes. Students learning to read English must learn strategies to manipulate phonemes by segmenting, blending, deleting, and so forth. In contrast, Spanish has 27 letters but only 22–24 phonemes, thereby making Spanish a very phonetically consistent language.
Words	Vocabulary is language-specific and must be taught in each language. However, cross-linguistic transfer can be facilitated through explicit instruction in cognates and common roots and affixes across English and Spanish.
Cultural Schema	Books and stories are products of culture and have assumptions, themes, and values embedded into them. Although certain themes transcend differences among languages and cultures, it is important that teachers explicitly teach the cultural background to successfully engage in text that is written in their second language or about a less familiar culture.
Story Structure	Story structures may vary language to language.

Adapted from the Center for Applied Linguistics (2016)

contrast, sound-symbol relationships in Spanish are very consistent, and children learning to read Spanish can read most text with a high level of accuracy much sooner. This distinction is not only important for dual-language and bilingual teachers to understand, but it is important for them to help parents and administrators understand as well for several reasons:

- Appropriate instructional levels of text will be different in English than in Spanish, which has implications for matching leveled text to readers for instructional purposes (see www.readingtapestry.com for a chart that aligns the DCC lectura leveling system with descriptions of English text).
- Teachers of dual language may need to explain to parents (and even administrators) discrepancies between reading in Spanish and reading in English.
- Accuracy will not be a strong predictor of reading comprehension in Spanish like it is in English, and students are likely to be able to decode beyond the level at which they can comprehend. Teachers need to be sure that they match Spanish text that students can read at a good rate, and with good comprehension.
- Teachers of early English reading will focus more on phonemic awareness, phonics, and sight words than is necessary for learning to read Spanish text.
- When learning letter/sound relationships, generally Spanish instruction starts with vowels whereas English starts with consonants.

Table 2.2 provides explicit comparisons between the foundational reading skills (print concepts, phonological awareness, phonics and word recognition, and fluency) at each of the early levels of the DCC lectura leveling instrument with their English counterparts.

By simply scanning the table, it is evident that students learning to read Spanish learn to decode more complex phonetic patterns at an early stage of development. Further, students learning to read English not only develop later, but are more reliant on using context to support the decoding and word recognition. Note that the levels are based on the Spanish and English versions of the CCSS (2012, 2010) and the TEKS (2017); more information about the DCC lectura levels is provided in chapter 4.

Table 2.2

Emergent Reader Stage of Development (Approximate Grade Level = Kindergarten)

	SPANISH		ENGLISH
ER1	• Diffwerentiates between print and pictures. • Recognizes that sentences are comprised of words separated by spaces and recognizes word boundaries. • Recognizes the difference between a letter and a printed word. • Develops oral language skills through listening, speaking, and discussion. • Develops stronger understanding of the connection between sounds and letters. • Identifies and matches the common sounds that letters represent. • Learns to follow text from left to right. • Learns to use one-to-one matching. • Learns some basic, high-frequency words.	**ER1**	• Demonstrates understanding of spoken words. • Recognizes a few high-frequency words (e.g., the, of, to, you). • Uses initial letter sounds to match word and picture. • Knows the long and short vowel sounds. • Recognizes and names of all uppercase and lowercase letters of the alphabet • Recognizes that spoken words are represented in written language by specific sequences of letters. • Demonstrates basic knowledge of one-to-one letter-sound correspondences by producing the primary sound or many of the most frequent sounds for each consonant.
ER2	• Identifies letters, words, and sentences. • Demonstrates concepts of print (e.g., title, front cover). • Knows that reading moves from top to bottom and left to right with return sweep. • Matches phrases and sentences to pictures. • Understands a few words of dialogue. • Recognizes and applies repeating language patterns. • Uses letter-sound relationships to decode one- and two-syllable words and multisyllabic words, including CV, VC, CCV, CVC, VCV, CVCV, CCVCV, and CVCCV. • Has expanded core of high-frequency words.	**ER2**	• Recognizes a few CVC words (dad, red, did, hot, sun). • Reads words repeated within the same text (e.g., is, it, I, am) • Follow words from left to right, top to bottom, and page by page • Understand that words are separated by spaces in print • Demonstrates understanding of spoken syllables and sounds (phonemes) • Recognizes and produces rhyming words • Associates the long and short sounds with the common spellings (graphemes) for the five major vowels • Reads common high-frequency words by sight (e.g., the, of, to, you, she, my, is, are, do, does)

ER3

- Identifies and produces rhyming words.
- Decodes words with silent h and consonant digraphs such as /ch/, /rr/, and /ll/.
- Begins to move smoothly across the printed page when reading
- Eyes are taking over the process of matching the spoken word to the printed word (removal of finger tracking).
- Develops a larger core of high-frequency words.
- Begins to use some expression when reading.
- Develops phrased reading (e.g., take a short breath after a comma)
- Notices dialogue and punctuation and reflects this with the voice.

ER3

- Recognizes and uses common VC patterns (e.g., -am, -at, -ot, -ug).
- Recognizes and uses some VCe patterns (-ace, -ade, -ake)
- Blends and segments onsets and rimes of single-syllable spoken words.
- Isolates and pronounces the initial, medial vowel, and final sounds (phonemes) in three-phoneme (consonant-vowel-consonant, or CVC) words. (This does not include CVCs ending with /l/, /r/, or /x/.)

ER4

- Processes texts with fewer repeating language patterns.
- Increases use of syllabic structures.
- Decodes common two-syllable words with any syllabic combination.
- Recognizes that new words are created when syllables are changed, added, or deleted
- Eyes can track print over two to six lines per page; finger pointing is rarely needed, if ever
- Continues increase of high-frequency words.
- Voice-print match is smooth and automatic.
- Notices and uses a range of punctuation and reads dialogue, reflecting the meaning through phrasing.

ER4

- Recognizes an increasing number of high-frequency words
- Reads plural nouns with (-s, -es)
- Counts, pronounces, blends, and segments syllables in spoken words
- Adds or substitutes individual sounds (phonemes) in simple, one-syllable words to make new words
- Distinguishes between similarly spelled words by identifying the sounds of the letters that differ.

Beginning Reader Stage of Development (Approximate Grade Level = Early First)

	SPANISH		ENGLISH
BR1	• Produces a series of rhyming words. • Recognizes spoken alliteration or groups of words that begin with the same simple syllable or initial sound. • Recognizes the change in spoken word when a specified syllable is added, changed, or removed • Segments spoken words into individual syllables • Left‑to‑right directionality and voice‑print match are automatic • Reads without finger pointing, bringing in finger only at point of difficulty. Recognizes names and high-frequency words by sight. • Oral reading demonstrates fluency and phrasing with appropriate stress on words	**BR1**	• Recognizes the distinguishing features of a sentence (e.g., first word, capitalization, ending punctuation) • Distinguishes long from short vowel sounds in spoken single-syllable words. • Decodes regularly spelled one-syllable words. • Reads words with common consonant blends (e.g., bl-, gr-, sp-). • Reads words with common consonant digraphs (e.g., ch-, ph-). • Reads words with double consonants in the middle or at the end.
BR2	• Blends spoken complex syllables, including sílabas trabadas, to form multisyllabic words. • Segments spoken words into syllables, including words with sílabas trabadas. • Manipulates syllables within words. • Decodes words with sílabas trabadas such as /bla/, /bra/, and /gla/; digraphs; and words with multiple sound spelling patterns such as c, k, and q and s, z, soft c, and x. • Left-to-right directionality and voice-print match are completely automatic. • Reads without pointing and with appropriate rate, phrasing, intonation, and stress. • Reads stretches of both simple and split dialogue.	**BR2**	• Orally produces single-syllable words by blending sounds (phonemes), including consonant blends. • Isolates and pronounces initial, medial vowel, and final sounds (phonemes) in spoken single-syllable words. • Segments spoken single-syllable words into their complete sequence of individual sounds (phonemes). • Recognizes and uses contractions with *not*, *am*, and *are*. • Reads words with VVC patterns (e.g., deer, good, room). • Recognizes and uses contractions with is and has.

Developing Reader Stage of Development (Approximate Grade Level = Late First–Second)

	SPANISH		ENGLISH
DR1	• Early reading behaviors now completely automatic. • Decodes words with silent h and words that use the syllables que-, qui-, gue-, gui-, güe-, and güi-. • Demonstrates appropriate rate, phrasing, intonation, and word stress. • Pays attention to basic punctuation and dialogue when reading aloud.	**DR1**	• Recognizes and uses contractions with will. • Solves words using letter-sound relationships from left to right (e.g., s-t-e-p). • Distinguishes long and short vowe s when reading regularly spelled one-syllable words. • Knows the spelling-sound correspondences for common consonant digraphs. • Decodes regularly spelled one-syllable words. • Reads words with inflectional endings. • Decodes two-syllable words with basic patterns by breaking the words into syllables.
DR2	• Decodes words with diphthongs such as /ai/, /au/, and /ei/. • Decodes contractions such as al and del. • Processes a great deal of dialogue and reflects it through appropriate word stress and phrasing.	**DR2**	
DR3	• Decodes three- to four-syllable words. • Uses knowledge of base words to decode common compound words. • Decodes words with common prefixes and suffixes. • Uses word solving strategies for complex spelling patterns, multisyllabic words, and words with inflectional endings, plurals, contractions, and possessives. • Interprets accent marks correctly.	**DR3**	• Decodes one-syllable words with a variety of patterns. • Recognizes 100+ high-frequency words. • Knows final -e and common vowel team conventions for representing long vowel sounds. • Uses knowledge that every syllable must have a vowel sound to determine the number of syllables in a printed word. • Reads grade-level text orally with accuracy, appropriate rate, and expression on successive readings. • Uses context to confirm or self-correct word recognition and understanding, rereading as necessary.

SPANISH		ENGLISH	
DR4	Quickly applies word-solving strategies for complex spelling patterns, multisyllabic words, and words with inflectional endings, plurals, contractions, and possessives.	**DR4**	Reads compound words
			Recognizes and uses contractions with *had* or *would*.
			Recognizes and uses homophones (e.g., nose, knows).
	Decodes multisyllabic words.		Distinguishes long and short vowels when reading regularly spelled one-syllable words.
	Oral reading reflects appropriate rate, stress, intonation, phrasing, and pausing.		Knows spelling-sound correspondences for additional common vowel teams.
			Decodes regularly spelled two-syllable words with long vowels.
			Reads grade-level text orally with accuracy, appropriate rate, and expression on successive readings.
			Uses context to confirm or self-correct word recognition and understanding, rereading as necessary.
DR5	Quickly applies word-solving strategies for complex spelling patterns, multisyllabic words, and words with inflectional endings, plurals, contractions, and possessives.	**DR5**	Knows spelling-sound correspondences for additional common vowel teams.
			Decodes words with common prefixes and suffixes.
	Decodes multisyllabic words with multiple sound spelling patterns such as c, k, and q and s, z, soft c, and x.		Identifies words with inconsistent but common spelling-sound correspondences.
	Decodes multisyllabic words with silent h and words that use the syllables que-, qui-, gui-, gue-, güe-, and güi-.		Recognizes and reads grade-appropriate irregularly spelled words.
	Decodes multisyllabic words with diphthongs and hiatus.		
	Decodes multisyllabic words decoding common abbreviations.		
	Decodes multisyllabic words with prefixes and suffixes.		
	Oral reading fully demonstrates all aspects of fluent reading.		

Transitioning Reader Stage of Development (Approximate Grade Level = Third)

	SPANISH		ENGLISH
• **TR1**	• Takes apart multisyllabic words and uses a full range of word solving skills.	• **TR1**	• Identifies and knows the meaning of the most common prefixes and derivational suffixes. • Decodes words with common Latin suffixes. • Decodes multisyllabic words.
• **TR2**	• Word solving is smooth and automatic with both oral and silent reading.	• **TR2**	• Reads grade-appropriate irregularly spelled words. • Reads grade-level prose and poetry orally with accuracy, appropriate rate, and express on on successive readings. • Uses context to confirm or self-correct word recognition and understanding, rereading as necessary.

National Governors Association Center for Best Practices & Council of Chief State School Officers, 2012; National Governors Association Center for Best Practices & Council of Chief State School Officers, 2010; Texas Administrative Code, 2017

HOW DOES THE SCIENCE OF
READING APPLY TO SPANISH?

As mentioned earlier in this chapter, the research that comprises the SoR is universal and spans many languages. Successful reading instruction weaves together structured and explicit word study with content knowledge building. DCC lectura's approach is founded in the SoR research, which blends the explicit and systematic phonics instruction that builds upon previously learned concepts.

Unlike other approaches to teaching reading, it is not assumed that students will naturally deduce these concepts on their own. Approaches to literacy instruction that do not use systematic phonics instruction will not meet the learning needs of at least 30% of students (National Reading Panel, 2000). In contrast, DCC lectura's research- and standards-based approach for teaching students to read Spanish supports deliberate teaching of skills and concepts with continuous student-teacher interaction.

SPANISH READING TAPESTRY

Teachers in the United States who are teaching emerging multilingual learners how to read Spanish text, must both be informed by key instructional practices that support the linguistic properties of Spanish and honor the value of learning how to read Spanish through linguistically and culturally authentic instruction.

Taking into consideration the aspects of the reading that are universal to all languages as well as the concepts that are specific to learning to read Spanish, DCC lectura has developed a cognitive framework for reading. The Spanish Reading Tapestry is anchored in an asset-based pedagogy that applies a systematic approach to biliteracy by weaving together a tapestry of the critical components of reading skills in Spanish.

Just as the threads of a tapestry have less meaning when they are isolated, the skills necessary to read Spanish have less meaning when they are isolated. As the threads of a tapestry are woven together, some colors and threads are more prominent than others, but if each thread is given the attention it needs at the appropriate time, beautiful, culturally authentic patterns will emerge.

The same is true of the stages of students' reading development. As the emerging multilingual students learn to read, certain skills and concepts will be the focus of instruction. Skills and concepts are never isolated but are interwoven through the context of culturally responsive and authentic text, allowing the beautiful, life-sustaining patterns of multilingual readers to emerge. The following section will present nine relevant instructional threads of reading that are organized by two strands: word recognition and language comprehension.

WORD RECOGNITION STRAND

Phonemic Awareness and Phonological Awareness

Phonemic awareness (PA), the ability to hear individual sounds in words and to identify particular sounds, is done through oral instruction and is a key component of teaching early readers of English. Instruction in Spanish literacy in the United States has been influenced by trends in English literacy research and instruction, most notably with an emphasis on phonemic awareness instruction as a precursor to reading.

Although instruction in Spanish phonemic awareness seems to have a positive effect on the development of spelling ability, both scholarly research and practical classroom experiences have found little direct evidence that an early focus on PA increases Spanish reading performance. Instead, in early-reading instruction of Spanish, phonemic awareness develops concurrently with learning to read. As students learn to identify Spanish words, the phonological codes assist with word identification and formation.

In contrast with phonemic awareness, which is the isolation of individual sounds, phonological awareness works with bigger units of words, such as syllables. Syllables are a key component to learning to read Spanish text and are the predictor of student success. Studies of phonemic awareness conducted with Spanish-speaking children have been used recently to confirm the different levels of phonological awareness that are relevant to the Spanish language (Defior et al., 2006). These levels include

- identification of phonemes in isolation,
- beginning and ending sounds and syllables, and
- intra-syllabic sounds.

The levels of phonological awareness impact the development of reading skills. Research also shows that strong phonological awareness in Spanish-speaking children is correlated with success in emergent spelling (de Manrique & Signorini, 1994). In other words, students who receive phonological awareness training are better able to spell words phonetically than students who do not receive the same instruction.

Oracy

James Britton is credited with saying, "Reading and writing flow on a sea of talk." This sentiment is especially important in the multiliteracy classroom. Oracy is the academic oral language required for reading and writing. Teaching oracy fosters the development of expressive language through structured dialogue and can be done in ways that put more intention behind how the teacher guides and organizes student talk.

Although oracy is important in every classroom, it is especially important in dual-language and biliteracy classrooms, where oracy instruction has many purposes. For example, when students gather for group work or discussions, they can brainstorm and review existing knowledge, extend their understanding of a topic, and express what they have learned to others (Norman, 1992).

Literacy routines in the multilingual classroom will be more effective when oracy is woven through *all* parts of literacy instruction, but it is especially important to establish routines that include oral language as an introduction to other literacy activities (Urow et al., 2019). Providing opportunities for students to engage in oral language will promote language development and can be used frequently at all grade levels (Texas Administrative Code, 2017).

Decoding

When readers decode words, a two-way processing system is engaged in which parts of the brain work together to recognize the letter patterns and identify the sounds associated with those patterns (Moats et al., 2016; Schwartz et al., 2007). Phonetic patterns are much more reliable in Spanish than in English because the letter/sound relationships are more consistent. The more consistent patterns affect the early readers' ability to decode text. Early readers of Spanish are able to decode with near 100% accuracy by mid-first grade.

In comparison, their same-age peers who are learning to read English decode with about 40% accuracy (Duke & Mesmer, 2019). Although decoding issues in Spanish are not as prevalent as issues of comprehension, DCC lectura supports systematic and explicit phonics instruction. The discrete phonics skills found in the stages of reader development structure (see chapter 3) and the leveling instrument (see chapter 4) are based on the CCSS en Espanol, the CCSS, and TEKS, as well as evidence-based instructional practices.

The phonics patterns in Spanish differ from English, so phonics instruction in each language should also differ. It is important that phonics instruction is not solely taught in isolation. All early readers need ample opportunities to apply newly learned foundational skills to text at the student's appropriate developmental stage.

Learning how to recognize isolated sounds and words is not sufficient for a developing reader. Phonics must be supported by meaning-making and context processing systems, or students are at risk of being able to recognize phonetic patterns and words but not associate those letters and sounds with the text's meaning (Moats, Glaser, & Tolman, 2016). Appropriate instruction of early readers of Spanish students includes

- initial phonics instruction through the context of authentic text, not in isolation;
- applying phonics through reading and writing of the content being studied; and
- using the el dictado to practice spelling patterns through a variety of methods (e.g., copying words/sentences, teacher modeling, working with sounds).

Most early readers of Spanish will respond to these methods, but teachers may observe that some students have gaps in their phonics skills and will need additional phonics support

- through small-group, skills-based instruction
- in groups based on their progress in applying foundational skills to text; or

SPANISH READING TAPESTRY

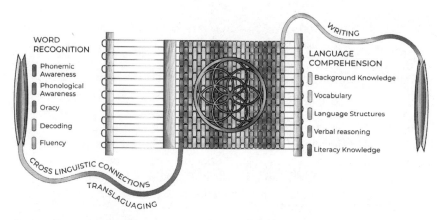

Figure 2.1. Spanish Reading Tapestry. Designed by Jose Balbin

- through an approach that analyzes spelling patterns in words and compares words with similar patterns.

Regardless of the language students are learning to read, the ultimate goal of learning phonics skills is to be able to apply phonetic patterns when reading and writing text. Application of phonics is crucial so teachers do not have the perception that the students' skills are more advanced than they are and inappropriately advance students to levels of text beyond their ability to comprehend.

Instead, students need ample opportunities to apply newly learned phonetic skills in their reading and writing. The sequence in which students will learn and apply Spanish phonics skills has been aligned to the stages of reader development and embedded as part of the foundational skills in table 2.2.

As Moats, Glaser, and Tolman (2016) point out, "students cannot comprehend text if they cannot read it accurately and fluently" (p. 37), so instruction that promotes automaticity and fluency are key components of developing successful readers. The teaching of high-frequency words in Spanish promotes comprehension by improving the automaticity of word recognition for early readers of Spanish.

As mentioned earlier in this chapter, a part of culturally sustaining teaching is recognizing that instructional practices that may be ideal in English are not always appropriate for Spanish. An example is the important, but different, roles high-frequency words play in the early literacy learning of Spanish and English.

In order to explore how high-frequency words differ in Spanish and English, it is important to first define two key terms:

- *high-frequency words*: words that occur often in the spoken and written language
- *non-decodable sight words*: words that don't follow the rules of spelling or phonics Students need to learn to recognize these words by sight.

The difference between high-frequency words and sight words is an important distinction, because it affects instructional practices. In Spanish, "sight words" do not exist like they do in English, so they do not need to be taught. Spanish phonics is much more consistent, so the language has *no* non-decodable sight words. In contrast, English phonetic patterns are not as consistent and not all words are decodable, making the memorization of sight words crucial for early readers of English. In fact, English sight words make the text more accessible; without knowing them, emerging readers simply will not learn to read.

Regardless of the language students are learning to read, the ultimate goal is to read fluently and with comprehension. Early readers who are struggling to read fluently will benefit from direct instruction and targeted practice on select high-frequency words in context.

To be clear, it is not imperative to teach Spanish high-frequency words to *all* students. Teachers can work with students who would benefit from increased automaticity of high-frequency words in a small-group setting, focusing on words that are slightly above the level that the student can read independently (see www.readingtapestry.com for DCC lectura's high-frequency word list). Learning these words will leverage the student's ability to read increasingly difficult text fluently.

Fluency

Reading fluency is critical to students becoming skilled readers. Despite its importance, reading fluency is often misunderstood and sometimes neglected in the classroom. When fluency is referred to in the context of school, it is most often meant as rate, yet fluency is much more than that. Fluency is the ability to read accurately, quickly, effortlessly, and with appropriate expression and meaning (Rasinski, 2003). To put it another way, when reading fiction orally, the reader should sound like he is telling a story. When reading nonfiction orally, the reader should sound like she is teaching something to someone.

In the Spanish Reading Tapestry, fluency is the bridge that takes students from the word recognition strand to the language comprehension strand. Apply the components of the word recognition strand in ways that develop automaticity, allow the students to remember what was read, and make connections to their background knowledge. If text is read in a laborious and halting way, the cognitive load of the reader is stalled in word recognition, making it difficult for the student to comprehend. Development of reading fluency begins at the earliest stages of reading and continues to be refined during the middle- and high-school years.

Given the reliable nature of Spanish phonetic patterns, one might expect that students learning to read Spanish would become fluent readers at an earlier age as well. However, a study that Álvarez-Cañizo et al. (2020) conducted found that Spanish and English reading fluency results are similar in both languages.

The key to developing reading fluency in both Spanish and English is to provide ample opportunities for both oral and silent reading practice, especially with nonfiction text (Álvarez-Cañizo et al., 2020; National Reading Panel, 2000). Reading practice during small-group instruction will provide students with explicit guidance and feedback from the teacher as they practice reading orally. Independent reading will provide students with opportunities to practice silent reading fluency. Simply put, the more students read, the more practice they will get, and the more fluent they will become.

LANGUAGE COMPREHENSION STRAND

Background Knowledge

Classrooms across the United States are composed of diverse populations of learners. Teachers who strive to make reading instruction asset based take a student-centered approach in which they first get to know and understand their students' word knowledge and world knowledge. The experiences, background knowledge, oral language, and vocabulary that students bring to the text will affect their success as readers.

Getting to know your students and the factors that make up their personal and family lives will help you make lessons more culturally sustaining, build relationships with students, and keep personal biases from influencing decisions. It can be as easy as finding the time to talk with your students and demonstrate a genuine interest in them.

Not all students will want to talk in front of their peers, so set aside time to talk to students one-on-one or in small groups to find out about their families, interests, and cultures. Show your students that you are interested in learning about them and that they bring value to your classroom community. Alternatively, teachers may choose to have their students take a student interest inventory and/or a family knowledge inventory to get to know them.

Culturally and linguistically diverse students need to connect with the curriculum to have a meaningful schooling experience. One way to provide asset-based reading instruction is to ensure that students have access to culturally relevant literature that represents their culture and language authentically and realistically. Involving students' families will help the teacher know about their students' cultures and respond to them in relevant, responsible ways.

Vocabulary

Background knowledge and vocabulary are closely related and are key components in reading comprehension. When considering stages of reader development and text levels, vocabulary is placed among meaning-making systems. Vocabulary is organized in the DCC lectura leveling instrument in this way because of the crucial role that vocabulary plays in the students' ability to comprehend text.

Academic vocabulary, for example, is taken into consideration when leveling text because typically the greater the number of academic words in a text, the greater the text complexity. If you would like more information, a table of how vocabulary becomes increasingly complex at each stage of reader development can be found at www.readingtapestry.com.

Language Structures

Research has shown that language development in a student's native language transfers to English and is foundational to cognitive development (Texas Administrative Code, 2017). Students who are becoming proficient in their home language(s) while learning to function in a new, additional language(s) benefit from an increased linguistic repertoire.

Grosjean's (1989) seminal study introduced the idea that the brains of multilinguals do not simply act as two monolinguals working side by side. Instead, the languages strengthen and support each other, enhancing the multilingual's ability to problem solve communicative situations (Escamilla, 2001). The multilingual classroom in which Spanish and English are taught has three linguistic spaces: Spanish, English, and cross-linguistic.

Cross-Linguistic Connections

Emergent multilinguals are constantly making connections and processing the similarities and differences between the languages that are part of their linguistic repertoire. In Cross-linguistic transfer, emergent multilinguals use their linguistic knowledge of one of their languages to leverage the learning of the other language(s).

Explicitly facilitating cross-linguistic connections is extremely important for students in dual-language and bilingual programs. These connections will help students start thinking and developing deeper metalinguistic awareness (Colon, 2019). For transfer to be maximized, cross-linguistic connections between the two or more languages must be taught explicitly while students engage in a contrastive analysis of the languages (Cummins, 2007).

A crucial aspect of establishing metalinguistic awareness is the systematic and purposeful use of strategies to build cross-linguistic connections in the classroom. Cross-linguistic connections involve students in learning by helping them make use of morphological, phonological, syntactic, semantic, and pragmatic differences and similarities between two or more languages. Cross-linguistic connections can also be made within languages, such as Spanish, that have a range of regional variants through the exploration of cultural impacts on regional dialects (Soltero, 2016).

Soltero (2016) states that these cross-linguistic connections may be in the form of scheduled lessons, but they can occur throughout the day as "teachable moments" during discussion, lessons, or when reading and writing. These provide teachers natural opportunities to guide students through comparison and contrast between the two languages.

In all multilingual classrooms, instruction needs to support the development of both languages and their cross-linguistic connections. In the classroom, both English and the program's target language have a specific purpose in the facilitation of language acquisition and biliteracy development (Eliason & Jenkins, 2012).

Dual-language teachers need to assign a color to each language and wear the color that corresponds to the language they are speaking. Using distinct colors for each language is a practical way to provide a visual cue to multilingual students about the language being spoken at any specific moment (Nettles, 2006). *Throughout* the program, not just in kindergarten, teachers should incorporate the use of colors to represent language.

Providing dual-language learners with opportunities to use language in both the spoken and written form supports their knowledge of the words they hear and the links between those words and the color-coding scheme. In other words, classroom walls, word walls, bulletin boards, and labels should represent the three linguistic spaces: the two languages of instruction and the cross-linguistic connection. Designate areas on the classroom walls for work in each language using colored bulletin-board material or borders. Once the linguistic spaces are color coded, consider how much of each language is shown and whether it fits the language allocation of your program model.

Translanguaging

Translanguaging is the act that bilinguals perform of accessing different linguistic features or various modes of what are described as autonomous languages to maximize communicative potential (García, 2009). Individuals who are multilingual draw on different language systems; the linguistic repertoire of emerging multilingual students taps into all languages available to them as they learn to read and write.

Translanguaging is an essential process to learn and to develop multilingualism. In the classroom, translanguaging may be used as a pedagogical tool that starts with building a linguistic space that allows for cross-linguistic connections. The multilingual classroom in which Spanish and English are taught has three linguistic spaces: Spanish, English, and cross-linguistic connections.

Having translanguaging spaces for teaching does not in any way negate the necessity for separate spaces in which children are asked to perform in one language or the other (Marrero-Colon, 2021). These separate linguistic spaces have been created so that the teacher understands which language to use and so that students have to broaden their language practices to meet the exigencies of conversation with monolinguals.

Just as teachers allocate time to distinct topic areas and establish connections among them, multilingual teachers in dual-language bilingual classrooms must similarly allocate a separate space to each of the languages while also making connections among the different language practices.

Translanguaging is an essential process to learn and to acquire bilingualism. In the classroom, translanguaging may be used as a pedagogical tool that starts with building a linguistic space that allows for cross-linguistic connections. Translanguaging as a pedagogical tool implies that the teacher is aware that the linguistic repertoire of the students extends beyond that of the language practices in the classroom, and he taps into that repertoire flexibly and actively to educate.

Translanguaging as pedagogy refers to any case in which the students' native language practices are used to leverage learning. In certain circumstances, the teacher organizes such translanguaging spaces actively and supports them via particular teacher-led activities. In other circumstances, the teacher permits such translanguaging spaces to unfold moment to moment as she engages bilingual students in learning and students themselves make decisions about their language usage.

Translanguaging occurs naturally in the classroom, but teachers may also assist translanguaging by purposefully teaching students to use all of their linguistic capacities. When the teachers' use of language is planned and purposeful, they enable students to participate and react to learning situations using all of the language elements accessible to them. Students are allowed to use their complete repertory of language, offering a safe space in which to develop their less-confident language.

Sánchez, García, and Solorza (2018) believe that language allocation methods that give greater flexibility to accommodate translanguaging practices might operate within current dual-language program models. To that purpose, they recommend that programs adopt a translanguaging allocation policy that contains three components:

1. Translanguaging Documentation

The translanguaging documentation component allows teachers to collect information that may be used to evaluate students' linguistic ability and academic performance holistically. Teachers, in particular, may examine and acknowledge the unique and dynamic ways their students are learning and using language via translanguaging documentation.

Rather than recording what students know and can do in just one language, teachers document what students know and can do when they employ all of their linguistic resources at the same time. This offers teachers a more comprehensive picture of each student's skills and suggestions for planning classes and learning activities that will further strengthen students' multilingualism. Teachers then may use this information to inform and differentiate their classroom teaching.

2. Translanguaging Rings

Translanguaging rings are instructional strategies that assist teachers in enhancing students' learning experiences by allowing them to build on their home languages. Teachers assist students in understanding how their languages are related. Teachers are creating translanguaging rings around their students as they adopt these instructional designs and strategies, allowing them to participate in activities that they would be unable to complete without support. Translanguaging rings are scaffolding techniques that enable teachers to use students' home languages as resources in learning the target language in the dual-language classroom.

3. Translanguaging Transformative Spaces

The construction of transformational translanguaging environments enables students to be themselves and talk as they do outside of school. Students' bilingual practices are acknowledged and promoted in these venues. Importantly, students are given the chance to critically analyze moments in their educational experiences in which their full language talents have been limited and delegitimized. This might be a really eye-opening experience for the students.

Although separate allocation of languages is necessary for many reasons, supporting them with translanguaging documentation, rings, and transformation allows for a more equitable and dynamic vision for teaching multilingual students (Garcia et al., 2017). In brief, when translanguaging is done purposefully in dual-language bilingual programs, teachers can help bilingual learners by building on all of their strengths and moving them ahead linguistically and academically in the two instructional languages.

Verbal Reasoning

Comprehension is the ultimate goal of reading. To achieve this goal takes all of the skills and strategies such as verbal abilities, phonics, and fluency working together to support the student's comprehension of the text (Moats,

Glaser, & Tolman, 2016). Spanish literacy instruction must consistently emphasize comprehension. Focusing on decoding text out of context and without keeping comprehension in mind may lead to using elevated text levels with students who are not ready for them.

Context also plays a key role in making meaning. The role of context in support of making meaning can be at the word, sentence, or text level. At the word level, context may help the reader determine the word's intended meaning. Context may also help readers catch miscues (Moats, Glaser, & Tolman, 2016). Context contributes to making meaning on a larger scale and when possible, teachers can build on the background and family knowledge that students bring with them to the classroom (Beeman & Urow, 2013).

Many studies (e.g., Dyson, 2008; Eeds & Wells, 1989; Jennings & Mills, 2009; Mercer, 2008) support children's use of their social context combined with their experiences to make meaning actively as they use language. Learning to read and write is a social process, and the social context of the classroom is key to making meaning. In the multilingual classroom, students use teacher and peer modeling to scaffold their learning (Turner, 1995; Turner & Paris, 1995), to create new understanding, and to refine the language they use to communicate (Wilkinson & Silliman, 2000).

Language is not just a vehicle for communication; it is also a method for constructing shared understanding and connections among the members of the classroom. It is well established that classroom discourse develops the literacy skills of students (Bloome, Power, Morton, Otto, & Shuart-Paris, 2005; Johnston et al., 2000; Nystrand, 2006; Wells & Claxton, 2002).

Literacy Knowledge

Understanding literacy concepts is crucial to the ability to comprehend increasingly complex text. As will be explained in chapter 4, the first phase of leveling text is to consider the surface systems related to book format, text structure, and genre. These surface systems are the foundation of text complexity.

Consider how very young children interact with books; they sit on a loved one's lap and observe pages being turned while they look at pictures and symbols. As children get a little older, they will turn the pages themselves, "read" the book, and mimic reading behaviors they have observed. These early reading behaviors eventually progress into knowledge about more complex genre structures. Literacy knowledge is an important part of the DCC lectura leveling system and is woven throughout all of the levels.

THE DCC LECTURA METHOD FOR
TEACHING READING IN SPANISH

Over decades of scholarly work, several methods to teach to read in Spanish have evolved. Instructional methods fall into three different categories: analytic, synthetic, or eclectic. Analytic methods start with the whole, at either the word or sentence level, and build meaning with an emphasis on language and less focus on systematic phonics. The synthetic methods start with the part and build with an emphasis on letter/sound relationships and systematic and explicit phonics instruction.

Generally speaking, eclecticism consists of taking the best components of many methods to form a new one. The eclectic approach, also known as mixed methods, is a form of reading instruction that integrates a range of techniques and methods for teaching language and responds to the aims and the learners' capabilities. The eclectic approach is considered both analytical *and* synthetic, because it correlates the spelling of each word with the thought it symbolizes. This strategy supports the teaching of reading and writing together.

The DCC lectura method is formed by taking the most valuable and significant components of the synthetic and analytical methodology to facilitate the learning of reading, writing, and comprehension. Our method takes advantage of both teaching and learning systems to create a more realistic process adapted to what students really need.

The DCC lectura method allows the achievement of broader objectives in the teaching of reading than the other, more specialized methods. The DCC lectura method selects the most valuable aspects of the other methods and applies them using asset-based pedagogical strategies.

The DCC Lectura Method Takes an Approach That

- *combines synthetic and analytical elements at all times.* Teachers show letters and sounds within the word, not in isolation. When the letter sound is taught, it is done with other representations or connections such as pictures, words, songs, or hand gestures. Instruction starts with the sound, then the syllable, then the word, and then using the syllables to form new words. The learning process is cumulative and sequential. A continuum of hierarchy is followed, from the simplest and most common sound to the most complex word.
- *promotes and motivates a learning environment that fosters interest and favors understanding.* It uses multisensory, hands-on learning and

intentional material. Text, tools, and resources are authentic, identity affirming, and motivating to students.

- *simultaneously teaches reading and writing*, which encourages linking the image of the letter to its sound. By teaching reading and writing together, each activity reinforces the other.

The DCC Lectura Method of Instruction

- *begins with oracy, and promotes the development of expressive language through structured dialogue*. Oracy development is expressly planned to precede any reading and writing skills.
- *follows a sequence in which students initially write vowels and subsequently consonants as emerging writers*. Vowels are taught first because they are consistent and regular. It is recommended that uppercase and lowercase letters be taught simultaneously.
- *follows a sequence in which letter names are not taught initially*; they are learned after students know that the letter sounds can form syllables. The way of learning letters is not based on the pronunciation of their name but in the learning, recognition, and discrimination of the articulation of their phonemes.
- *teaches students to begin reading in Spanish by first learning the five vowel sounds*. Spanish reading and writing instruction starts with the vowels and then proceeds to consonants to form syllables. Understanding that there are strong vowels (a-e-o) and weak vowels (i-u) determines separation of words into syllables. In Spanish the emphasis is on learning to form and read syllables. Once learners thoroughly know the vowel sounds and can form syllables, they are capable of decoding most words.
- *follows the introduction of vowels with the consonants that are easiest for students to distinguish and to blend with vowels*. Consonants are introduced by their degree of phonetic difficulty and frequency of use: m, p, s, l, b, l, t, d, r, c, n, f, v, j, g, ch, ñ, v, ll, qu, z, h, y, x, k, w. They are presented one at a time and practiced with consonants that have been learned previously.
- *encourages students to explore words by first becoming skilled at reading words made up of basic open syllables*; then with words that are composed of closed syllables, as well as words with consonant blends, diphthongs, triphthongs, and hiatus. Finally, syllables with silent letters are introduced.
- *teaches that accent marks are critical for conveying information about how words are spoken*. Accents emphasize important points. Each word in Spanish has an accent, a stressed syllable; however, these are not always indicated by an accent mark. Accents are critical because they

influence the meaning of words, not just in terms of writing and spelling, but also in terms of the diacritic accent. For students, understanding how vowels and syllables are produced is critical to using accents
appropriately.

- *allows for cross-linguistic connections to occur in two ways in the
classroom—strategically planned lessons and teachable moments.*
Natural, spontaneous opportunities for cross-linguistic connections will
be initiated by the students as they make connections and will provide
teachers with opportunities to support and guide students in comparing
and contrasting languages.

- *is an authentic and systematic process for assessing, monitoring, and
supporting as a language-specific sequence of skills is followed.* Use
DCC lectura's leveling instrument and assessments to consider the student's needs and skill levels. It employs diagnostic teaching, whereby
the teacher observes the student's progress during instruction and creates
an individualized path for learning.

Chapter 3

Stages of Reader Development

Reading is not walking on the words; it's grasping the soul of them.

—Paulo Freire

KEY POINTS IN CHAPTER 3

- The seven stages of reader development give teachers a framework for the stages that readers progress through as they become more proficient readers.
- Books are leveled in order to appropriately match readers with text. We level books, *not* students.
- Getting to know your students as readers is built on a foundation of the teacher/student relationship.
- Students within any given grade level will be at varying stages of reader development depending on their backgrounds, language proficiency, and experience as a reader.
- The quick check is a screener that assists teachers in determining the approximate level of text that would be a good initial match for their readers.
- Once an initial level of text is matched with a reader, the formative assessment of reader characteristics can be used to fine-tune the level used for instruction.

INTRODUCTION TO STAGES OF
READER DEVELOPMENT

As teachers who work with early literacy students know, most children follow a pattern of reading behaviors as they learn to read. Early reading behaviors begin with phonemic and print awareness. Students become more aware of the symbols and icons in their environment and are beginning to "read" familiar and predictable books through memorization and by imitating the reading behaviors that are modeled for them. Following these early reading behaviors are other predictable patterns of reading development that appear at distinct stages.

Researchers have broken down the stages of development into anywhere from five to seven stages and have used a variety of labels to identify each stage (Chall, 1983; Fountas & Pinnell, 1996; Richardson, 2016). These developmental stages of learning to read give teachers a framework for the stages that readers progress through as they become more proficient. The DCC lectura design includes seven distinct stages, which are based on CCSS en Espanol, the TEKS, and evidence-based instructional practices.

Overview of DCC Lectura's Seven Stages of Reader Development

Table 3.1 is an alignment chart that shows how the seven stages of reader development are aligned with the 21 levels of the DCC lectura leveling instrument and the approximate grade level.

It is important to note that students within any given grade level will be at varying stages of reader development depending on their backgrounds, language proficiency, and experience as a reader. The grade level listed in the table is the grade level at which students should be exposed to a particular level of text in whole-group instruction. (See www.readingtapestry.com for the complete descriptions of the reader characteristics broken down by the 21 levels.)

LEVELING BOOKS, NOT STUDENTS

All too often the reading levels that were designed and intended to be used to level text (e.g., Fountas & Pinnell, DRA) are used to level readers. It is vital to keep in mind that the purpose of leveling text is to have appropriate materials to use during small-group instruction. Reading levels are not a part of the student's identity; and the intention is *never* to level the students but to

Table 3.1

Approx. Grade Level	Stage of Reader Development	Levels of Text	Summary of Reader Characteristics
Pre-K	Red: Pre-Reader	PR	At the pre-reader stage of development, the key reader characteristics relate to an interest in books and an awareness of the concepts of print that are crucial in early literacy.
K	Orange: Emergent Reader	ER1, ER2, ER3, ER4	At the emergent reader stage of development, the key reader characteristics relate to phonics skills that begin with letter sounds and progress to the ability to decode two-syllable words with any syllabic combination. At this stage, developing increasingly fluent reading behaviors is crucial. Fluency work at this stage begins with left-to-right directionality until the ability to track print with the eyes for a smooth and automatic voice-print match emerges. Learning high-frequency words will help the process of reading with increasing fluency. The emergent reader is being introduced to comprehension strategies and is able to access them with adult assistance.
1	Yellow: Beginning Reader	BR1, BR2	At the beginning reader stage of development, the key reader characteristics relate to a developing understanding of the structures and characteristics of informational text. At this stage, phonological awareness has developed, and students have the ability to manipulate syllables of spoken words. Students are less dependent on picture clues, and vocabulary increases rapidly as students learn 2–3 words per day.
1 & 2	Pink: Developing Reader	DR, DR2, DR3, DR4, DR5	At the developing reader stage, readers are developing their understanding of characteristics of genre, often through the deep connection between oracy and reading. Early reading characteristics are now automatic; and by the end of this developmental stage, students will demonstrate all aspects of fluent reading as they master most decoding skills. Readers are beginning to understand more complex stories and will begin to read early chapter books. Content-specific vocabulary is beginning to be introduced, and readers are developing the ability to comprehend

Approx. Grade Level	Stage of Reader Development	Levels of Text	Summary of Reader Characteristics
			informational text independently. The developing reader stage is pivotal, and it is important that all reader characteristics are balanced and developed together. A focus on phonics without context, meaning-making systems, and self-monitoring may result in students being matched with text that they are able to decode but unable to comprehend.
3	Purple: Transitioning Reader	TR1, TR2	At the transitioning reader stage, readers become more independent in the use of key reader characteristics such as self-monitoring. Word solving becomes unconscious and automatic, using syntax and the grammatical functions of language to understand the text. The focus transitions from the surface structures (e.g., phonics) to the deeper structures of comprehension. The transitioning reader is able to use background knowledge and text evidence to make inferences and learn new information.
4	Green: Developing Independence Reader	DIR1, DIR2	As genre and text types become more sophisticated, the reader characteristics at the developing independence stage focus on attending to self-monitoring that will help the reader navigate unfamiliar text types and genres. Using vocabulary strategies to understand content and academic vocabulary become increasingly important to support the increased need to comprehend nonfiction text.
5–12	Blue: Independent Reader	IR1, IR2, IR3, IR4, IR5	At the independent reader developmental stage, the reader's ability to navigate and comprehend text will depend mostly on the reader and not on aspects specific to the text. Readers at this developmental stage have most of the key reader characteristics needed to read all levels of text. Appropriate text-to-reader match is dependent on the readers' experiences, vocabulary, interests, and the sophistication with which they can analyze the author's craft in a wide range of genres and forms.

match a students' current stage of reader development with the level of text that appropriately challenges them during small-group instruction. As many have asserted (Fountas & Pinnell, 2019; Serravallo, 2018), levels were never intended to be a child's label or identity.

Teachers need a way to identify and describe their students' reading behaviors, so they often use text levels to describe or label students. DCC lectura addresses the need for a system to describe the pattern of reading behaviors that most children follow as they learn to read by providing teachers with a research-based framework for thinking about students' reading behaviors.

The stages of reader development were designed to be respectful of each student's biliteracy journey while still maintaining the rigor of grade-level standards. Teachers simply identify the reader characteristics that they have observed in their students to determine the students' stages of reader development (specifically, how to do that is described later in this chapter). Once a student's stage of reader development has been identified by the teacher, DCC lectura provides a system for matching readers with the level of text that will help them progress in a developmentally and linguistically appropriate way (see chapter 5).

DCC lectura encourages teachers always to begin with the reader in mind by first considering the student's stage of reader development. The stages are aligned with grade levels, so teachers can be assured that they are maintaining the rigor and standards for the grade level(s) they teach. Multiple text levels align with each stage of reader development to provide teachers with a specific, scaffolded approach to instruction.

GETTING TO KNOW YOUR STUDENTS AS READERS

Getting to know your students as readers extends beyond simply listening to them read and asking them what types of books they like. As Muhammad (2020) so aptly stated, "identities are multi-layered and shaped by the social and cultural environment as well as by literacy practices" (p. 49). Teachers need to find ways to get to know how their students self-identify beyond how their identities are perceived by the school. Teachers should consider the intersectionality of the different types of identities that their students have including racial, ethnic, linguistic, gender, cultural, and community.

Getting to know the factors that make up their personal and family lives will help teachers take an asset approach during lessons and build relationships with their students. In addition to identity, considering factors such as socioeconomic status, family makeup, the educational expectations and goals that a family has for the child, student interests and experiences will enhance the teacher/student relationship and provide opportunities to make the learning experiences more personalized and better meet the students' needs.

The DCC lectura leveling instrument matches readers to text. Students are not a level, nor does one specific level meet all of the needs of a reader. A level DR4 text, which is a solid instructional fit for a developing reader, may be too frustrating for that same reader to have an enjoyable literary experience as she sits down to read at bedtime. A range of text levels will be appropriate for an individual child and will depend on the reader's experience, language, and purpose.

Getting to know your students as readers and finding their stages of reader development while using the DCC lectura method involves a process with three general steps: build a relationship, do a quick check, and assess formatively.

Build a Relationship

Get to Know the Student as a Person and as a Reader

Because the learner is at the center of this work, so is the relationship that is built between learner and instructor. To most accurately assess the needs of the reader and to truly match text to reader, the instructor must have developed a relationship with the learner. Relationships are a prerequisite to learning.

Fisher, Frey, and Hattie (2016) discuss the benefits of teacher/student relationships, and their research has determined that a positive teacher/student relationship can have a significant effect on a student's learning. They stress that for students to achieve high levels of literacy, teachers have to "develop positive, trusting relationships with students, all students" (p. 13). In *Cultivating Genius* (2020), Muhammad suggests many questions to find out about the histories of the students' families and cultures. Suggested questions include asking

- what languages the students speak,
- how the students see themselves and their lives,
- the role that language and literacy play in the students' lives, and
- how students practice literacies at home and in their community.

You may find or develop questions related to these themes, or you may find that conversations about identity, language, and literacy happen organically, but it is most important to listen to and trust the children as they share their identities and themselves with you.

Conduct an Interest Inventory

As Beeman and Urow (2013) so aptly stated, "with understanding of the reader, the teacher can look for texts that are culturally relevant and interesting" (p. 91). A simple way to gain an understanding of the reader is to conduct an interest inventory. Giving students an interest inventory is a time-tested common practice. Many versions of interest inventories can be found online or in professional books; the one that has been provided below asks questions not only about the students' reading preferences, but also a bit about their language, family, and experiences.

Student Interest Inventory

1. Which language do you mostly use with your brothers and sisters? Or if you don't have brothers and sisters, what language do you mostly use at home?
2. What is your favorite thing to do with your family?
3. In what ways does your family or community share stories? Do you read stories? Write stories? Tell or listen to stories?
4. How would you learn more about something that interests you?
5. How do you feel about reading?
6. What are some books that you've read lately (or that have been read to you)?
7. What are some things that you do to help out at home?
8. What is something that you would like to learn or read about?

Learn about the Students' Family, Background, Culture, and Histories

Vélez-Ibáñez and Greenberg (1992) termed the phrase "funds of knowledge" to describe the collective knowledge acquired through the experiences and cultural resources of the family members. Their position argues that the funds of knowledge could be used to understand the cultural backgrounds of students and to inform classroom instruction. By getting to know families through conversations, interviews, and relationship building, teachers learn about the funds of knowledge their students and their families bring to the school community, then use the learned information to connect the funds of knowledge to curricular standards (Gonzalez, Moll, & Amanti, 1992, 2002, 2007).

Building a relationship with students' families will take some time, and teachers need a way initially to get to know their students well enough to match the collective knowledge of their families with text that may engage and interest them. To serve the initial purpose of getting to know students as readers, the funds of knowledge concept has been applied to interest inventories for families. The family knowledge inventory is provided below.

Family Knowledge Inventory

1. Which language(s) are used in your home? Which languages does your child speak?
2. What are some important family and cultural traditions?
3. What are some important values that you share with your child?
4. What is something you would like us to know about your family and your family's history?
5. What are some favorite things you do or places you go as a family?
6. What are some of the ways your family engages in literacy (reading, writing, speaking, listening)?
7. Which jobs/occupations do the members of your family have?
8. What are some specific topics that the members of your family know a lot about (e.g., gardening, law, fishing)?

Quick Check

Teachers need to equip students in dual-language and bilingual classrooms with the tools they need to be able to weave together structured and explicit word study with building content knowledge. As mentioned earlier in this chapter, the seven stages of reader development give teachers a structure for understanding and identifying the predictable patterns of reading development and the distinct stages at which their students are performing.

Emerging multilingual students will be at varying stages of reader development depending on their backgrounds, Spanish language proficiency, and experiences as a reader. It is often difficult for a teacher to know exactly what level of text to put in the hands of a reader she is getting to know. After getting to know the students, how they self-identify, and the role that Spanish plays in their lives, the quick check provides the teacher with either a starting point for instruction or an understanding that further assessment will be needed.

The quick check uses a combination of word lists, short books or passages, and reading rate to determine an appropriate text level to match with the reader. Much like an eye chart is used by an eye doctor to determine the approximate sharpness of a patient's vision, the quick check is designed as a screener that assists teachers in determining the *approximate* level of text that would be a good initial match for their readers.

How to Begin the Quick Check:

- For kindergarten, first-, or second-grade students
  1. Give the student the high-frequency word lists found at www. readingtapestry.com:
     - Kindergarten: Word List 1
     - First Grade: Word List 2
     - Second Grade: Word List 3
  2. Using the results of the quick check word list, select the level of text the student should read to assess comprehension. Emergent and beginning readers will read a quick check foldable book. (Reproducible versions of the books and directions on how to fold them can be found www.readingtapestry.com.) Students who are developing readers will read a quick check passage (also available at www.readingtapestry.com).
- For third-, fourth-, or fifth-grade students (or students who read the quick check word list with 100% accuracy)
  1. Beginning with the first level in the stage of reader development of the student's grade level, read the characteristics for that stage. If it fairly accurately describes your student's reading proficiency, that is the level at which you will begin the quick check. If not, work up or down to find the stage that seems to describe your student. If you are still trying to get to know the student as a reader, begin with the stage that aligns with the grade level and adjust as necessary.
  2. Provide the student with a quick check passage at the selected level and follow the directions on the quick check passages.

Notes about Quick Check:

The quick check is not designed to be used with pre-readers (PR) or students who are reading at an instructional level equivalent to a fifth-grade level (IR2) because

- key reader characteristics at the pre-reading stage relate to promoting an interest in books and an awareness of the concepts of print that are crucial in early literacy. Students are not yet reading words. The instructional focus should be on early literacy skills (see levels of text and reader characteristics for more information).
- a reader's ability to navigate text complexity levels IR3 and above depends largely on the reader and not on aspects specific to the text. Readers at this developmental stage have most of the key reader characteristics needed to read all levels of text. Appropriate text-to-reader

match is dependent on the readers' experiences, vocabulary, interests, and the sophistication with which they can analyze the author's craft in a wide range of genres and forms.

Formative Assessment of Reader Characteristics

The DCC lectura formative assessment of reader characteristics (FARC), which can be found at www.readingtapestry.com, is a tool that helps teachers observe and record the reader characteristics of students as they read and discuss leveled text. As you meet with students during small-group instruction or while conferring, the FARC can be used for two purposes.

1. When you have first matched a student with leveled text, the FARC can be used to observe the reader engage with the selected level of text and reassure you that you have matched the student with the level most appropriate for instruction.
2. When working with students as they progress in their reading skills, the FARC can be used to observe and record the reader characteristics as you work with students during small-group instruction or while conferring.

CONTINUING TO KNOW YOUR STUDENTS AS READERS

As you work with your students and they continue to learn and grow as readers, you will be reading with them, conferring with them, and tracking their progress. The FARC should be used as an ongoing assessment tool to gauge students as they progress through the stages of reader development and are able to tackle increasingly complex text. Teachers are welcome to reproduce the FARC and are encouraged to manage the use of the FARC in the way(s) that are most efficient and meaningful to them. However, the following suggestions provide ways in which the FARC can be used to keep track of progress and to guide differentiated instruction.

- Use a three-ring binder with a divider for each student. Print and copy the sections of the FARC that align with the stages of reader development for your students. As students demonstrate each skill or strategy, highlight their personalized FARC, moving them on to more complex text when appropriate.

- Make one copy of the FARC to use for your entire class. As students demonstrate each skill or strategy, put the students' initials next to that strategy. Advance students to more complex text when appropriate.

Chapter 4

Leveling Text

Better is possible. It does not take genius. It takes diligence. It takes moral clarity. It takes ingenuity. And above all, it takes a willingness to try.

—Atul Gawande

KEY POINTS IN CHAPTER 4

- Leveled text is a system teachers can use to select the books that will be the most effective match for the readers and/or instructional purpose.
- DCC lectura's leveling instrument is made up of three systems of leveled text: surface, linguistic, and meaning-making.
- When selecting high-quality Spanish text, consider text that is authentic, culturally relevant, diverse, and culturally responsive.
- Multiple text levels align with each stage of reader development to provide teachers with a specific, scaffolded approach to instruction.

INTRODUCTION TO LEVELED TEXT

Using a progression of standards-based skills and strategies is a key component of teaching reading in dual-language and bilingual programs. Leveled text can be used as a tool to offer students appropriately challenging materials that match their current stage of reading development and provide teachers with a way to tailor their instruction to meet the reader's needs. This chapter will introduce DCC lectura's leveling instrument and will provide a simple and practical method for leveling Spanish language books.

It is vital to keep in mind that the purpose of leveling text is to have appropriate materials to use during small-group instruction. The intention is *not* to level the students but to match students' current stage of reader development, as described in chapter 3, with the level of text that appropriately challenges them during small-group instruction. The following bullet points, adapted from Fountas and Pinnell (2017), provide an overview of the many ways that leveled text can be used appropriately as well as the ways it is commonly misused or misunderstood.

What Leveled Text IS . . .	What Leveled Text IS NOT . . .
• a key component of a Spanish adapted science of reading (SoR) approach	• any part of a student's identity
• a way to match text to readers	• a way for teachers, schools, or districts to label students
• targeted material for small-group instruction and conferring	• a component of reading for entertainment or pleasure
• an efficient way for teachers to determine text complexity	• one specific level that meets all of the needs of a reader
• an efficient way to select effective books for small-group instruction	• a grade to be communicated on a report card
• a tool to help determine whether students are proficient in grade-level standards	• a guideline for *students* to select their books for independent reading
• a way to mark reading growth over time	• a way for students or parents to compare the progress of one student with another
• a flexible guideline for *teachers* to follow when assisting with the selection of books for independent reading	
• a tool to help determine whether students need additional supports through intervention or enrichment	

When considering a leveling instrument, it is important to understand the purpose and intent of the levels. The two primary purposes for determining the level of a text are to assign levels of complexity to text and to match readers to text for the purposes of instruction.

1. Assign levels of complexity to text

Understanding the qualitative and quantitative aspects of a text will help teachers:

• find texts that are a good fit for small-group instruction;

- guide students as they learn how to navigate increasingly complex text; and
- unravel the complexities of reading to set learning goals, scaffold reading skills, and provide targeted and actionable feedback.

2. Match readers to text

The primary purpose for a leveling instrument is to match readers to text. It is unlikely that one specific level will meet all of the needs of a reader. One particular level of text that is a solid instructional fit for a developing reader may be too frustrating for that same reader to have an enjoyable literary experience. Instead, a range of text levels will be appropriate for an individual child depending on the reader's experience, interests, Spanish language proficiency, and purpose.

INTRODUCTION TO DCC LECTURA'S LEVELING INSTRUMENT

DCC lectura's leveling instrument allows teachers to efficiently and accurately determine the levels of Spanish text. DCC's leveling instrument is comparable to other systems in English (e.g., Fountas & Pinnell, DRA) in that it provides teachers with the text levels to be used for instruction. However, DCC lectura's leveling instrument has the added benefit of being based on the Spanish version of the CCSS and the TEKS.

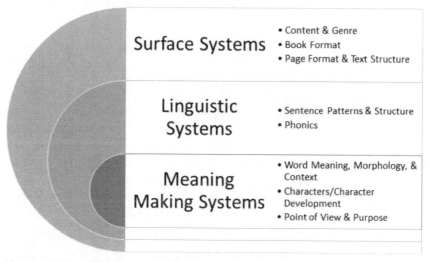

Figure 4.1. Three Basic Systems of DCC lectura Leveling Instrument

The leveling instrument includes detailed descriptions of text based on three basic systems: surface, linguistic, and meaning-making (Keene, 2006). The systems, represented in figure 4.1, each include characteristics of text that together create a detailed and comprehensive structure for the culturally responsive leveling of Spanish language books.

The surface systems are the first consideration in leveling books. These systems provide information about the layout and content of books (e.g., words per page, genre). Surface systems provide a general sense of the text complexity (almost literally judging a book by its cover).

The linguistic systems provide approaches to reading text that are distinct from one language to another (Kenne, 2006). The linguistic systems in the leveling instrument are specific to the patterns and structures that are distinct to the Spanish language (e.g., grapho-phonic patterns, the Spanish accent mark).

The meaning-making systems include the increasingly complex and technical words that will be used as the text level increases and the information that is necessary to comprehend and process the text. Together, the three basic systems provide teachers with the information they need to determine the levels of Spanish books.

Types of Text

Teachers will want to select quality Spanish text for students not only for instructional purposes but also as a means of elevating Spanish. You will want to show students that quality text with good illustrations is published in Spanish and not just English. Quality books draw the reader in and teach children how to love and respect books. Printed books provide a visceral experience that is not shared when reading digital text.

As access to technology increases and is provided to students at a very young age, the window that educators have to expose students to text is becoming smaller and smaller. With this in mind, take a moment to consider how to select high-quality Spanish text and the types of text that teachers may encounter as they search for the most effective books to use with their students. You will also want to read Heather Robertson-Devine's piece (see appendix C) on Spanish book collections for more information about selecting authentic Spanish text and literacy ecosystems.

As teachers choose texts for their students using DCC lectura's leveling instrument, key questions related to each of the three basic systems should be asked. These questions will help teachers determine whether a given text is instructionally appropriate and culturally relevant for their student(s).

Questions Teachers Should Ask Related to Surface Systems:

- Based on observations of my students' reading behaviors and running records, which stage of reading development provides my students enough of a challenge during small-group reading instruction to allow them to learn and grow as readers without frustrating them?
- Is the genre and topic/content of the text something with which my student is familiar?
  - If so, a good instructional match for the students may be at the higher end of their stage of reading development.
  - If not, a good instructional match may be at the lower end of their stage of reading development.
- Based on the illustrations and topic, does this book seem to be a responsive representation of my students?
- Based on the illustrations and topic, does this book seem to be culturally relevant?

Questions Teachers Should Ask Related to Linguistic Systems:

- Which language am I teaching the students to read?
- Based on the language and specific words and phrases used, is this book culturally representative of the students in my classroom?
- Is this text an authentic representation of the language I am teaching my students to read?

Questions Teachers Should Ask Related to Meaning-Making Systems:

- Is this text authentic literature? If not, do I have a specific reason or purpose for selecting this text? Is it worthy of my students?
- Is the content/topic of this book culturally relevant?
- In considering the other books that I have used this year, does this book contribute to the equitable representation of the students in my classroom?

DCC LECTURA'S LEVELING PROTOCOL

DCC lectura's leveling instrument allows teachers to determine the levels of authentic Spanish text. The protocol guides teachers through analyzing three basic systems of text: surface, linguistic, and meaning-making systems so they can find the appropriate level of text to be used for instruction. Teachers who are new to leveling text may need approximately 10 to 15 minutes per book to follow the protocol, but as they become more familiar with the characteristics of each level, they will find that it takes as little as five minutes per book.

When leveling text, keep in mind that the leveling instrument includes characteristics of text that are typical of a given level and that not every characteristic of text at a given level will appear in every book at that level. In addition, the leveling instrument protocol is somewhat subjective, and different people examining the same book may come to different conclusions about what is the best designated level of a book. As teachers, you can work together to discuss the text features of books and how to best match leveled books to readers in your classrooms to maximize instructional effectiveness.

Step 1: Select Text

In selecting quality Spanish text for instruction, consider

- Is this text authentic literature?
- Does the text align with the instructional purpose(s)?

Step 2: Leveling Selected Text

The protocol for leveling text occurs in three phases. It may be helpful to refer to table 3.1, which aligns the stages of reader development with the levels of text and the approximate grade level when learning how to level books.

Phase 1: The first phase will look at the surface structures of the text, which will determine the basic text level without taking into consideration language and content. This phase should be considered the initial scan of the book much like a doctor may look at a patient's appearance to determine wellness before running any diagnostic tests. The text characteristics at this phase are more descriptive in the less complex text levels. This is because the surface systems are a greater indicator of an early reader's ability to navigate the text than for an independent reader.

Start Phase 1 by estimating the grade level at which the book could appropriately be used to teach reading skills and strategies. Then read the description of the surface systems at the stage of reading development that corresponds with that grade level (see table 4.1). For example, if you believe

Table 4.1: Phase 1 of Leveling Selected Text

Approx. Grade Level	Level	Surface Systems
Pre-K	PR	• Simple informational texts, storybooks, or poems • Nonfiction text that includes simple directions • Picture books with simple pictures that clearly depict word(s) on the page • Pictures depict real-life objects • Clear labels used in nonfiction text • Directions in nonfiction text are clearly supported by diagrams or pictures • One to two words per page
K	ER1	• Simple informational book, or a simple genre such as storybook or poetry • Clear, simple illustrations that heavily support the text • Nonfiction text with labeled diagrams • Nonfiction text with labeled pictures and illustrations • Nonfiction text with titles and simple graphics • Three to six words per page • One line of text on each page
K	ER2	• Simple informational book, or a simple genre such as storybook or poetry • Simple illustrations that support patterns the text • Nonfiction text with pictures with a strong relationship to words in the text • Three to seven words per page • Two or more lines of text on each page • Simple dialogue
K	ER3	• Simple informational book, or a simple genre such as storybook or poetry • Simple illustrations that support patterns in the text • Clear relationship between illustrations and the story in which they appear • Two to five lines of text on each page
K	ER4	• Resource material such as a picture dictionary • Simple nonfiction text with words that name actions, colors, shapes, locations, and so forth • Illustrations clearly relate to the text • Illustrations in fiction text that clearly depict the story • Nonfiction text with illustrations that help the student to clarify word meanings • Two to five lines of text on each page • Some sentences turn over to the next line • Some text with punctuation that indicates dialogue

Approx. Grade Level	Level	Surface Systems
1	BR1	• Simple informational book • Simple genres of fiction (e.g., animal fantasy, realistic fiction) • Some information provided by pictures or other illustrations and some information provided by the words in a text • Some text has illustrations that match figurative language • Two to eight lines of text on each page • Sentences may continue onto the next page • Some texts may have print that has varied placement on the page • Text may have full range of punctuation
1	BR2	• Simple informational texts • Simple genres of fiction (e.g., very simple retellings of traditional tales, simple plays) • Some information provided by pictures or other illustrations and some information provided by the words in text • More details in illustrations • Illustrations may be more abstract and not directly support the print • Three to eight lines of text on each page • Some nonfiction books include multiple parts (e.g., glossary, index)
1	DR1	• Informational texts • Simple genres (e.g., traditional literature, folktales) • Complex illustrations depicting multiple ideas • Some informational texts with a table of contents and/or a glossary • Some informational texts use diagrams to show information • Three to eight lines of text on each page • Slightly smaller print • Text has full range of punctuation
1	DR2	• Informational texts • Increased variety of genres common to children's books (e.g., fairy tales, folktales) • Complex illustrations depicting multiple ideas • Informational texts include common text features (e.g., headings, tables of contents, glossaries, electronic menus, icons) • Books are increasing in length. • Eight to 16 pages of print • Italics may be used to indicate unspoken thought
1	DR3	• Simple genres of most types • Some easy illustrated chapter books • Summarizes simple narrative nonfiction • Some simple biography • Some persuasive text • Characteristics of genre are evident and support predictions • Some unusual formats, such as letters or questions followed by answers • Texts of eight to 16 pages • Nonfiction text includes text features and simple graphics

		• Easy chapter books have 40 to 60 pages
		• Smaller print
		• Some longer (10 words or more) and more complex sentences
		• Sentences may carry over to two or three lines, and some over two pages
		• Text features and structures may support predictions
2	DR4	• Informational books or slightly more complex genres (e.g., some biographies of familiar people)
		• Images and illustrations help to clarify text
		• Beginning chapter books have supporting illustrations
		• Forty to 75 pages
		• Many lines of print on a page
2	DR5	• Slightly more complex informational texts
		• Slightly more complex genres of fiction (e.g., some biographies of familiar people)
		• Increasing variety of texts (short fiction texts, short informational texts, and longer narrative texts that have illustrations and short chapters)
		• Images and illustrations help to clarify text and support comprehension
		• Beginning chapter books
		• Informational texts include various text features (e.g., captions, bold print, subheadings, glossaries, indexes, electronic menus, icons)
		• Print and graphic features are used to achieve specific purposes
		• Varied organization in nonfiction text formats (question/answer, boxes, legends, etc.)
		• Nonfiction text includes organization and resources to look for information (e.g., title, table of contents)
		• Sixty to 100 pages of print
		• Some fiction text has a great deal of dialogue within a story
3	TR1	• Informational texts or increasingly complex genres (e.g., mysteries, fantasies)
		• Poetry uses rhyme scheme, meter, and graphical elements, of all types such as punctuation and capitalization in poems across a variety of poetic forms
		• Images or illustrations are used to contribute to what is conveyed in words
		• Chapter books
		• Nonfiction may include organizational patterns such as compare and contrast
3	TR2	• Most genres including dramas, poetry, or myths
		• Narratives have more elaborate plots
		• Images or illustrations are used to contribute to what is conveyed in words
		• Fiction may be based on concepts that are distant in time and space and reflect diverse cultures
		• Informational texts include text features and search tools
		• Variety of structures in informational text (e.g., chronology, comparison, cause/effect, problem/solution)
		• Sixty to 100 pages of print

Approx. Grade Level	Level	Surface Systems
4	DIR1	• Genres include biographies of lesser-known people, humor, historical fiction, collections of short stories, and science fiction) • Minimal illustrations in literary text, most of the content carried by print rather than pictures • More difficult layout of informational text, and some fiction text, with denser format
4	DIR2	• Increasingly varied genres such as fiction with elaborate plots, legends, hybrids, and myths • Nonfiction genres include argumentative text • Variety of structures in informational text (e.g., chronology, comparison, cause/effect, problem/solution) • Minimal illustrations in literary text, most of the content carried by print rather than pictures • Nonfiction text includes features that support understanding such as sections, tables, graphs, time lines, bullets, numbers, and bold and italicized font • Nonfiction may contain a variety of complex graphics, often more than one on a page
5	IR1	• Increasingly varied genres such as tall tales, folktales • More complex narrative structures (e.g., story-within-a story, flashback) • Informational text includes elements such as the controlling idea or thesis with supporting evidence; features such as introduction, foreword, preface, references, or acknowledgments to gain background information; and organizational patterns such as definition, classification, advantage, and disadvantage • Minimal illustrations in literary text, most of the content carried by print rather than pictures • Increasingly difficult layout of informational texts, with dense content and format
6–7	IR2	• More complex genres • Specific types of poetry (sonnet, soliloquy) • Some poetry uses sound devices and figurative language in a variety of poetic forms • Drama includes structures such as character tags, acts, scenes, and stage directions • Informational text includes structures such as the central idea with supporting evidence; features such as insets, time lines, and sidebars to support understanding; and organizational patterns such as logical order and order of importance • Most fiction texts with minimal illustrations or no illustrations other than the cover
8	IR3	• Expanding types of complex genres • A wide variety of complex graphics that require interpretation (photos with legends, diagrams, labels, cutaways, graphics, maps)

| 9–10 | IR4 | • Expanding complex genres including satire, epic, and ballad
• Poetry uses rhyme scheme, meter, and graphical elements of all types including epic and ballad, such as punctuation and capitalization in poems across a variety of poetic forms
• Informational text includes characteristics and structural elements such as the controlling idea or thesis with supporting evidence; features such as references or acknowledgments, chapters, sections, subsections, bibliography, tables, graphs, captions, bullets, and numbers; and organizational patterns that support multiple topics, categories, and subcategories
• Unusual text organizations (e.g., flashbacks) |
| 11–12 | IR5 | • All genres
• Informational text includes characteristics and structural elements such as the controlling idea or thesis with supporting evidence; features such as footnotes, endnotes, and citations; and multiple organizational patterns within a text to develop the thesis
• Books with variation in color to communicate mood (e.g., sepia, black-and-white, color)
• May use graphical elements such as punctuation and line length in poems across a variety of poetic forms such as epic, lyric, and humorous poetry |

the book you selected to level "looks" like a third-grade book, then read how the surface systems are described at TR1 and TR2. Continue going up and down the levels until you have found the level at which the surface systems of the book most closely match the description in table 4.1.

Phase 2: The second phase will look at the linguistic systems of the book, including sentence patterns and structure. Begin with table 4.2 at the level determined by Phase 1, then adjust up or down based on the surface system

Table 4.2: Phase 2 of Leveling Selected Text

Level	Linguistic Systems
PR	• Words only, no sentences
ER1	• Repeating language patterns • Short, predictable sentences
ER2	• Introduction of dialogue (assigned by "dijo" in most cases) • Some text with rhyming words • Text with one- and two-syllable words and multisyllabic words, including CV, VC, CCV, CVC, VCV, CVCV, CCVCV, and CVCCV
ER3	• Text with one- and two-syllable words and multisyllabic words, including CV, VC, CCV, CVC, VCV, CVCV, CCVCV, and CVCCV • Text may include words with silent h and consonant digraphs such as /ch/, /rr/, and /ll/
ER4	• Fewer repetitive language patterns • Simple dialogue (some split dialogue) • Many sentences with prepositional phrases and adjectives • Increased use of syllabic structures; common two-syllable words with any syllable combination

Level	Linguistic Systems
BR1	• Some texts with sequential information • Some longer or more complex sentences with more than 10 words
BR2	• Wide variety in words used to assign dialogue to speaker • Increasing amount of dialogue • May include words with diphthongs such as /ai/, /au/, and /ei/; may include contractions such as al and del
DR1	• Some longer texts with repeating longer and more complex pattern including clauses and embedded phrases • Some complex letter-sound relationships may include words with silent h and words that use the syllables que-, qui-, gue-, gui-, güe-, and güi-
DR2	• May include words with diphthongs such as /ai/, /au/, and /ei/
DR3	• Longer sentences • Texts include three- to four-syllable words • Texts include common compound words • Texts include words with common prefixes and suffixes • Texts include words with complex spelling patterns, multisyllabic words, and words with inflectional endings, plurals, contractions, and possessive
DR4	• Varied placement of subject, verb, adjectives, and adverbs in sentences • Increasingly more complex sentences • Texts with complex spelling patterns, multisyllabic words, and words with inflectional endings, plurals, contractions, and possessives
DR5	N/A
TR1	• Longer (more than 15 words) and more complex sentences
TR2	• Longer (more than 15 words) and more complex sentences
DIR1	• Some lengthy, complex sentences containing prepositional phrases, introductory clauses, and lists of nouns, verbs, or adjectives
DIR2	• Longer (more than 15 words) and more complex sentences • May include palabras agudas, graves, esdrújulas, and sobresdrújulas (words with the stress on the last, penultimate, and antepenultimate syllable and words with the stress on the syllable before the antepenultimate)
IR1	• Wide range of declarative, imperative, or interrogative sentences
IR2	N/A
IR3	N/A
IR4	• Some very long sentences (more than 30 words)
IR5	N/A

characteristics. Not every level of text has descriptors in the linguistic systems, and the text characteristics at this phase are more descriptive in the early developmental stages than the later stages, which are more dependent on Phase 3 to determine level.

Phase 3: The third phase will use table 4.3 to look at the meaning-making systems of the book, including word meaning, theme, character development, and point of view. Begin at the level determined by Phase 2, then adjust up or down based on the meaning-making systems' characteristics. The text

Table 4.3: Phase 3 of Leveling Selected Text

Level	Meaning-Making Systems
PR	• All vocabulary is familiar to children
ER1	• Almost all vocabulary is familiar to children • Text includes core high-frequency words
ER2	• Almost all vocabulary is familiar to children • Simple story patterns with predictable outcomes • Nonfiction text that includes steps in a sequence
ER3	• Some words that are unfamiliar to children • Story lines and themes that are familiar to most children • Some text with a clear author's purpose
ER4	• Some words may be unknown to children but are related to more familiar words (por ejemplo: saber que el zapatero es la persona que vende o arregla zapatos) • Expanded core of high-frequency words • Text includes words that help the reader visualize • Story includes predictions that are supported by text features and illustrations
BR1	• Some words may be unknown to children but are related to more familiar words (por ejemplo: saber que el zapatero es la persona que vende o arregla zapatos) • Full range of high-frequency words • Stories include a central message or lesson • Illustrations and details are used to describe key ideas in the text • Author's purpose is supported by text structure in some texts • Author may use print and graphic features to achieve specific purposes
BR2	• Words and phrases in literary text include words that suggest feelings or senses • Stories include a central message or lesson • Characters have traits that are typical for the genre of the text • Text includes multiple characters that are crucial to the story • Some first- and third-person texts • Author's purpose is supported by text structure
DR1	• Words in nonfiction text include some content-specific words that are not supported by illustrations or pictures • Stories include a central message or lesson • Fiction text has more complex story lines and ideas
DR2	• Sentences include context clues to support word meaning • May include some complex language and vocabulary • Reflexive verbs • Stories include a central message or lesson
DR3	• Frequently occurring roots and affixes • Text includes words that help the reader visualize • Stories include central message or lesson • Main character(s) in fiction text demonstrate traits through their actions • Story may be told by different characters/narrators at various points in a text • Text includes text features that support predictions • Persuasive text makes it clear what the author is trying to persuade the reader to think or do

Level	Meaning-Making Systems

DR4
- Some bolded words to indicate key words
- Some compound words (por ejemplo: pasar, pasatiempo; sacar, Sacapuntas; bien, bienvenidos)
- Book's central message or lesson is clearly based on the story's events
- Connections are made between and among historical events, scientific ideas or concepts, or steps in technical procedures in a nonfiction text
- Some traits or feelings of the main character may not be obvious
- Story may be told by different characters/narrators at various points in a text

DR5
- Frequently occurring affixes added to lesser-known words (por ejemplo: feliz-infeliz, contar-recontar)
- Words and phrases that are used to create rhythm and meaning in a story or poem
- May include affixes including re-, pre-, -ción, and ísimo/ísima to determine the meaning of words and subsequently use the newly acquired words
- Inclusion of antonyms, synonyms, idioms, and homographs in context
- May include homographs, homophones, and commonly confused terms such as porque/porqué/por qué/por que, sino/si no, and también/tan bien
- Text features, characteristics of genre, and structures support predictions
- Nonfiction text includes explicit characteristics and structures including the central idea and supporting evidence
- Nonfiction text includes clear organizational patterns such as chronological order and cause and effect
- Nonfiction text is made more complex through the relationships or interactions between and among two or more individuals, events, ideas, or concepts in a historical, scientific, or technical text
- Characters in a story respond to major events and challenges
- Characters interact in ways that convey information about their characteristics
- Characters' different points of view are depicted

TR1
- One to two academic vocabulary words/phrases per page
- Frequently occurring affixes added to lesser-known words (por ejemplo: feliz-infeliz, contar-recontar)
- Words and phrases that are used to create rhythm and meaning in a story or poem
- Stories include a central message, lesson, or moral
- Traits and actions of characters in a story contribute to the sequence of events
- Strong relationships between and among historical events, scientific ideas or concepts, or steps in technical procedures in a nonfiction text are conveyed through language that pertains to time, sequence, and cause/effect

TR2
- One to two academic vocabulary words/phrases per page
- Words and phrases with literal and nonliteral meanings (por ejemplo: Tomar medidas. Está lloviendo a cántaros)
- Real-life connection between words and their use (por ejemplo: describen a personas que son simpáticas o serviciales)
- Text includes descriptive words, some complex content-specific words, and some technical words

- Words that have shades of meaning that describe states of mind or degrees of certainty and the use of the subjunctive mode to express doubt
- Nonfiction texts include underlying organizational structures (description, compare and contrast, problem and solution, cause and effect)
- Stories include subtle ideas
- Literary and nonfiction text includes a theme or central idea that emerges, shaped and refined through specific details over the course of the text
- Plot elements, including the use of foreshadowing and suspense, may be used to advance the plot
- Setting may influence character and plot development
- Rhetorical devices, such as direct address and rhetorical questions; and logical fallacies, such as loaded language and sweeping generalizations, may be used
- Narrative nonfiction may include both fact and opinion
- Expository text may include both fact and opinion

DIR1
- Words with prefixes and suffixes
- Three to five academic vocabulary words/phrases per page
- May include figures of speech
- Language may include imagery, literal and figurative language such as simile and metaphor, and sound devices such as alliteration and assonance to achieve specific purposes
- General academic and domain-specific words and phrases, including those that signal precise actions, emotions, or states of being (por ejemplo: emocionado, afligido, eufórico) and that are basic to a particular topic (por ejemplo: vida silvestre, conservación y en peligro de extinción cuando se habla de la protección de los animales)
- Story, drama, or poem includes a theme
- Story may include multiple causes and effects
- In-depth characters, with both good and bad traits, who change and develop over time
- Points of view of the narrators or characters are clearly conveyed
- Author's point of view or purpose in a nonfiction text is clearly conveyed

DIR2
- Many complex content-specific words in nonfiction, mostly defined in text, illustrations, or glossary
- Some use of Greek and Latin roots
- Common Greek and Latin affixes (por ejemplo: telégrafo, fotografía, autógrafo)
- Simple similes and metaphors (por ejemplo: tan bonito como una fotografía)
- Common idioms, adages, and proverbs
- General academic and domain-specific words and phrases (por ejemplo: emocionado, afligido, eufórico)
- Words and phrases that are basic to a particular topic (por ejemplo: vida silvestre, conservación y en peligro de extinción cuando se habla de la protección de los animales)
- Some words and phrases that allude to significant characters found in mythology (por ejemplo: Hércules)
- May include words with affixes, such as mono-, sobre-, sub-, inter-, poli-, -able, -ante, -eza, -ancia, and -ura; and roots, including auto, bio, grafía, metro, fono, and tele
- May include idioms, homographs, and homophones such as abrasar/abrazar

Level	Meaning-Making Systems

- May include homographs, homophones, and commonly confused terms such as porque/porqué/por qué/por que, sino/si no, and también/tan bien
- May include a story, drama, or poem including a theme
- May include anecdotes
- Specific information is used to explain events, procedures, ideas, or concepts in a historical, scientific, or technical text

IR1
- Three to five general academic or domain-specific vocabulary words/ phrases per page
- Many words with affixes (prefixes and suffixes)
- Simple similes and metaphors (por ejemplo: tan bonito como una fotografía)
- Some idioms, adages, and proverbs
- Context provides clues to indicate meaning of words or phrases (e.g., cause/ effect relationships and comparisons in text)
- Story, drama, or poems include a theme that is conveyed through particular details
- Characters interact in ways that convey information about their characteristics
- Nonfiction text is made more complex through the relationships or interactions between and among two or more individuals, events
- Ideas, or concepts in a historical, scientific, or technical text
- Characters in plays are developed through dialogue and staging
- Points of view of the narrators or characters are well developed
- Author's point of view or purpose in a nonfiction text is clearly conveyed

IR2
- Six to 10 academic vocabulary words/phrases per page
- Words used in regional or historical dialects; some words from languages other than Spanish
- Many words with affixes (prefixes and suffixes)
- The position or function in a sentence provides clues to the meaning of some words
- Relationship between particular words provides clues to the meaning of each of the words (por ejemplo: relaciones de causa/efecto, parte/todo, elemento/categoría)
- Words and phrases with figurative, connotative, and technical meanings
- Literary works may include rhymes and other repetitions of sounds (e.g., alliteration) that contribute to meaning
- Text may include words with affixes, such as trans-, super-, anti-, semi-, -logía, -ificar, -ismo, and -ista; and roots, including audi, crono, foto, geo, and terr
- Text may include idioms, adages, and puns
- Text may include homographs, homophones, and commonly confused terms such as porque/porqué/por qué/por que, sino/si no, and también/ tan bien

- Includes palabras agudas, graves, esdrújulas, and sobresdrújulas (words with the stress on the last, penultimate, and antepenultimate syllable and words with the stress on the syllable before the antepenultimate)
- Language such as hyperbole, stereotyping, and anecdote may contribute to the text's voice
- Literary text includes a theme or central idea developed over the course of the text and conveyed through particular details
- Nonfiction text has two or more central ideas developed over the course of the text
- The plot of literary text unfolds in a series of episodes and includes characters who respond or change as the plot moves toward a resolution
- Key individuals, events, or ideas are introduced, illustrated, or elaborated upon in a variety of ways (e.g., through examples or anecdotes)
- Elements of a story or drama interact (e.g., setting shapes the characters or plot)
- Nonfiction text includes interactions between individuals, events, and ideas in a text (e.g., how ideas influence individuals or events, or how individuals influence ideas or events)
- Points of view of the narrators or characters are well developed and contrast with one another
- Author's point of view or purpose in a nonfiction text is clearly conveyed, and the author's position is distinguished from those of others

IR3
- Long, multisyllabic words requiring attention to roots to read and understand
- Includes analogies or allusions to other texts
- Figurative language such as metaphor and personification used to achieve a specific purpose
- Literary devices may include omniscient and limited point of view
- Analyzes how the author's use of language contributes to mood and voice
- May use rhetorical devices and logical fallacies
- May determine the meaning and usage of grade-level academic Spanish words derived from Greek and Latin roots including metro-, grafo-, scrib-, and port-
- Text may differentiate between and use homographs, homophones, and commonly confused terms such as porque/porqué/por qué/por que, sino/si no, and también/tan bien
- Literary text includes a theme or central idea developed over the course of the text and conveyed through particular details
- Nonfiction text has two or more central ideas developed over the course of the text
- Particular lines of dialogue or incidents in a story or drama propel the action, reveal aspects of a character, or provoke a decision
- Nonfiction text makes connections among and distinctions between individuals, ideas, or events (e.g., through comparisons, analogies, or categories)

Level	Meaning-Making Systems

- Differences in the points of view of the characters and the audience or reader (e.g., created through the use of dramatic irony) create such effects as suspense or humor
- Author's point of view or purpose in a text is explicitly acknowledged, and author responds to conflicting evidence or viewpoints

IR4
- Eleven to 15 academic vocabulary words/phrases per page
- Words that are archaic, come from regional dialect, or from languages other than Spanish
- Sophisticated use of figures of speech (e.g., euphemism, oxymoron)
- Words and phrases are used in the text to create a cumulative impact on meaning and tone (e.g., how the language sets a sense of time and place; how it sets a formal or informal tone; how the language of a court opinion differs from that of a newspaper)
- Literary and nonfiction text includes a theme or central idea that emerges, shaped and refined through specific details over the course of the text
- Plot elements, including the use of foreshadowing and suspense, may be used to advance the plot
- Setting may influence character and plot development
- Rhetorical devices, such as direct address and rhetorical questions; and logical fallacies, such as loaded language and sweeping generalizations, may be used
- Complex characters (e.g., those with multiple or conflicting motivations) develop over the course of a text, interact with other characters, and advance the plot or develop the theme
- Characters' qualities may influence events and resolution of the conflict
- Authors use rhetoric to advance their point of view or purpose in a nonfiction text

IR5
- Sixteen to 21+ academic vocabulary words/phrases per page
- Words and phrases with figurative and connotative meanings that impact meaning and tone, including words with multiple meanings or language that is particularly fresh, engaging, or beautiful (Incluir a Cervantes, así como a otros autores de lengua española)
- May use context within or beyond a paragraph to clarify the meaning of unfamiliar or ambiguous words
- May use words that name actions, directions, positions, sequences, and locations
- May use multiple-meaning words, homographs, homophones, and commonly confused terms correctly
- May include words and phrases with figurative, connotative, and technical meanings that are used to refine the meaning of a key term or terms over the course of a text (por ejemplo: cómo define Bolívar "país" y "patria" en La carta de Jamaica)

- Literary and nonfiction text includes two or more themes or central ideas that interact and build on one another over the course of the text
- Stories may include nonlinear plot development such as flashbacks, foreshadowing, subplots, and parallel plot structures
- Dramatic action is developed through the use of acts and scenes in plays
- May use literary devices, including multiple points of view and irony
- May use language to contribute to the mood, voice, and tone
- May use rhetorical devices, such as analogy and juxtaposition; and logical fallacies, such as bandwagon appeals and circular reasoning
- Text includes a complex set of ideas or sequence of events that develops over the course of the text
- Author conveys point of view in ways that require the reader to distinguish what is directly stated in a text from what is meant (e.g., satire, sarcasm, irony, or understatement)
- Author's point of view or purpose in a text is conveyed through rhetoric that is particularly effective; style and content contribute to the power, persuasiveness, or beauty of the text

characteristics at this phase become more detailed and complex beginning at the developing reader stage. When you have completed Phase 3, you have leveled the text.

Integrity Check of Leveled Text

As mentioned earlier in this chapter, regardless of the leveling system teachers are using, leveling text is a somewhat subjective process, and different people examining the same book may come to different conclusions about what is the best designated level of a book. Keep in mind that due to the quantitative features of books, this is not an exact science. Leveling text complexity depends on three components: qualitative dimensions, quantitative dimensions, and reader and task (National Governors Association Center for Best Practices, 2010). Only the quantitative dimensions of text (e.g., word length, sentence length) are measurable objectively.

The other two components are subjective measures such as the text's language complexity and the readers' purpose. Due to the mostly subjective nature of this process, together as teachers you can discuss, compare, and learn about leveling texts together. One way to do this is by following a few simple steps (outlined in figure 4.2) to do an integrity check of the texts(s) that are leveled.

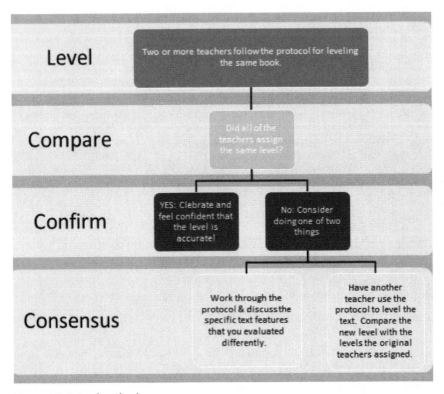

Figure 4.2. Integrity Check

Chapter 5

Examples of Leveled Text

Learning to recognize our differences, our diversity, can be an act of respect and admiration, and not one of separation. Diversity for me involves making room to hear other voices, and to recognize the connections that bind us together.

—Yuyi Morales

KEY POINTS IN CHAPTER 5

- When leveling text, it is important to keep in mind that the leveling instrument includes characteristics of text that are typical of a given level, and not every characteristic of text at a given level will appear in every book at that level.
- The leveling instrument protocol is a somewhat subjective process, and different people examining the same book may come to different conclusions about what is the best designated level of a book.
- We encourage teachers to work together, to discuss the text features of books, and to know that the true purpose of the leveling system isn't just to assign a level to a book but to match books to readers to maximize instructional effectiveness.
- When leveling books, refer to the examples in this chapter and compare them to the books being leveled.

Using the step-by-step guide for how to level books provided in chapter 4, every teacher will have the ability to offer students appropriately challenging materials that match their current stage of reading development. While leveling books, it is important to keep in mind the subjective nature of leveling authentic text and to use the integrity check process as a way to compare and discuss the characteristics of texts with colleagues.

The intent of chapter 5 is to take that guidance a step further and provide exemplars of each level. During the process of leveling books, teachers can refer to the titles that are provided as examples in this chapter and compare the books they are leveling with the books that DCC lectura considers to be at a given stage of reader development.

THE STRUCTURE OF THIS CHAPTER

This chapter is organized by the overarching reader stage of development and provides titles of exemplar texts for each stage. Then within each stage a table includes the text characteristics for that level organized by the three systems of leveled text: surface, linguistic, and meaning-making.

Note that text characteristics in bold font are of particular importance for that level. Bolded characteristics are significant to a given level because they indicate that they are distinct and are likely to be helpful when leveling text. Starting at level BR1, the bold features can be used to set goals with students who are navigating a new level of text, or to prioritize teaching points for small-group instruction.

When leveling Spanish books, it is important to remember always to begin with the reader in mind and select books that are culturally responsive, authentically representing and validating the students' cultures. Having access to and reading high-quality books about people of their own culture can engage students' emotions and encourage them to find literature that is meaningful to them. The titles we have provided are simply examples of types of books found at each stage of development. When selecting books for your own students, the true guiding factors for text selection will be your students' cultures and interests.

Levels of Text

Table 5.1: Text Characteristics of Pre Reader Level

Pre-Reader Exemplars
Números by Menena Cottin *Lotería* by Patty Rodriguez and Ariana Stein *La Catrina* by Patty Rodriguez and Ariana Stein

Pre-Reader	
Surface Systems	• Simple informational texts, storybooks, or poems • Nonfiction text that includes simple directions • **Picture books with simple pictures that clearly depict word(s) on the page**

- Pictures depict real-life objects
- Clear labels used in nonfiction text
- Directions in nonfiction text are clearly supported by diagrams or pictures
- **One to two words per page**

Linguistic Systems   • **Words only, no sentences**

Meaning-Making Systems   • **All vocabulary is familiar to children**

Table 5.2: Characteristics of Emergent Reader Levels

Emergent Reader Exemplars
¿Para qué sirve un koala? by Javier Bizarro Benítez and José Antonio Bizarro Benítez *La princesa zanahoria* by Paulina Jara *Cuando nos hayamos comida el planeta* by Alain Serres *Julieta salió a buscar* by Renato Cisneros

Emergent Reader 1 (ER1)	
Surface Systems	• Simple informational book, or a simple genre such as a storybook or poetry • **Clear, simple illustrations that heavily support the text** • Nonfiction text with labeled diagrams, pictures, and/or illustrations • Nonfiction text with titles and simple graphics • **Simple Sentences** • **Three to six words per page** • **One line of text on each page**
Linguistic Systems	• **Repeating language patterns** • **Short, predictable sentences**
Meaning-Making Systems	• Almost all vocabulary is familiar to children • **Text includes core high-frequency words**

Emergent Reader 2 (ER2)	
Surface Systems	• Simple informational book, or a simple genre such as a storybook or poetry • Simple illustrations that support patterns the text • Nonfiction text with pictures with a strong relationship to words in the text • **Two or more lines of text on each page** • Some simple dialogue
Linguistic Systems	• Introduction of dialogue (assigned by "dijo" in most cases) • Some text with rhyming words • Text with one- and two-syllable words and multisyllabic words including CV, VC, CCV, CVC, VCV, CVCV, CCVCV, and CVCCV
Meaning-Making Systems	• Almost all vocabulary is familiar to children • **Simple story patterns with predictable outcomes** • Nonfiction text that includes steps in a sequence

Emergent Reader 3 (ER3)

Surface Systems	• Simple informational book, or a simple genre such as a storybook or poetry • Simple illustrations that support patterns in the text • Clear relationship between illustrations and the story in which they appear • **Two to five lines of text on each page**
Linguistic Systems	• Text with one- and two-syllable words and multisyllabic words including CV, VC, CCV, CVC, VCV, CVCV, CCVCV, and CVCCV • Text may include words with silent h and consonant digraphs such as /ch/, /rr/, and /ll/
Meaning-Making Systems	• Some words that are unfamiliar to children • **Story lines and themes that are familiar to most children** • Some text with a clear author's purpose

Emergent Reader 4 (ER4)

Surface Systems	• Resource material such as a picture dictionary • Simple nonfiction text with words that name actions, colors, shapes, locations, and so forth • Illustrations clearly relate to the text • Illustrations in fiction text that clearly depict the story • Nonfiction text with illustrations that help the student to clarify word meanings • Two to six lines of text on each page • **Some sentences turn over to the next line** • Some text with punctuation that indicates dialogue
Linguistic Systems	• **Fewer repetitive language patterns** • Simple dialogue (some split dialogue) • Many sentences with prepositional phrases and adjectives • Increased use of syllabic structures • Common two-syllable words with any syllable combination
Meaning-Making Systems	• Some words may be unknown to children but are related to more familiar words (por ejemplo: saber que el zapatero es la persona que vende o arregla zapatos) • Expanded core of high-frequency words • Text includes words that help the reader visualize • **Story includes predictions that are supported by text features and illustrations**

Table 5.3: Text Characteristics of Beginning Reader Levels

Beginning Reader Exemplars

Hablemos con el agua by Macmillan Castillo Infantil
La oruga impaciente by Ross Burach
Punto y reímos by Carol Libenson Svachka and Susana Rosique
Quizás algo hermoso by F. Isabel Campoy and Theresa Howell

	Beginning Reader 1 (BR1)
Surface Systems	<ul><li>Simple informational book</li><li>Simple genres of fiction (e.g., animal fantasy, realistic fiction)</li><li>the words in a text</li><li>Some text has illustrations that match figurative language</li><li>Two to eight lines of text on each page</li><li>Sentences may continue onto next page</li><li>**Some texts may have print that has varied placement on the page**</li><li>Text may have full range of punctuation</li></ul>
Linguistic Systems	<ul><li>Some texts with sequential information</li><li>**Some longer or more complex sentences—more than 10 words**</li></ul>
Meaning-Making Systems	<ul><li>Some words may be unknown to children but are related to more familiar words (por ejemplo: saber que el zapatero es la persona que vende o arregla zapatos)</li><li>Full range of high-frequency words</li><li>Stories include a central message or lesson</li><li>Illustrations and details are used to describe key ideas in the text</li><li>Author's purpose is supported by text structure in some texts</li><li>**Authors may use print and graphic features to achieve specific purposes**</li></ul>
	Beginning Reader 2 (BR2)
Surface Systems	<ul><li>Simple informational texts</li><li>Simple genres of fiction (e.g., very simple retellings of traditional tales, simple plays)</li><li>Some information provided by pictures or other illustrations and some information provided by the words in text</li><li>More details in illustrations</li><li>**Illustrations may be more abstract and not directly support the print**</li><li>Three to eight lines of text on each page</li><li>**Some nonfiction books include multiple parts (e.g., glossary, index)**</li></ul>

Beginning Reader 2 (BR2)	
Linguistic Systems	• Wide variety in words used to assign dialogue to speaker • **Increasing amount of dialogue** • May include words with diphthongs such as /ai/, /au/, and /ei/; may include contractions such as al and del
Meaning-Making Systems	• Words and phrases in literary text include words that suggest feelings or senses • Stories include a central message or lesson • **Characters have traits that are typical for the genre of the text** • **Text includes multiple characters that are crucial to the story** • Some first- and third-person texts • Author's purpose is supported by text structure

Table 5.4: Text Characteristics of Developing Reader Levels

Developing Reader Exemplars

Ecología hasta en la sopa by Mariela Kogan
El ladrón de letras by Ethel Villarreal Cabello
Se me ha roto el corazón by Elef Yemenici
¿De donde eres? by Yamile Saied Mendez
La princesa Sara no para by Margarita del Mazo and Jose Fragoso

Developing Reader 1 (DR1)

Surface Systems	• Informational texts • Simple genres (e.g., traditional literature, folktales) • **Complex illustrations depicting multiple ideas** • Some informational texts with a table of contents and/or a glossary • Some informational texts use diagrams to show information • **Slightly smaller print** • Text has full range of punctuation
Linguistic Systems	• **Some longer texts with repeating longer and more complex pattern including clauses and embedded phrases** • Some complex letter-sound relationships in words; may include words with silent h and words that use the syllables que-, qui-, gue-, gui-, güe-, and güi-
Meaning-Making Systems	• **Words in nonfiction text include some content-specific words that are not supported by illustrations or pictures** • Stories include a central message or lesson • Fiction text has more complex story lines and ideas

Developing Reader 2 (DR2)

Surface Systems	• Increased variety of genres common to children's books (e.g., fairy tales, folktales) • Complex illustrations depicting multiple ideas • Informational texts include common text features (e.g., headings, tables of contents, glossaries, electronic menus, icons) • **Books are increasing in length** • **Eight to 16 pages of print** • Italics may be used to indicate unspoken thought
Linguistic Systems	• May include words with diphthongs such as /ai/, /au/, and /ei/
Meaning-Making Systems	• Sentences include context clues to support word meaning • **May include some complex language and vocabulary** • Reflexive verbs • Stories include a central message or lesson

Developing Reader 3 (DR3)

Surface Systems	• Simple genres of most types • **Some easy illustrated chapter books** • Easy chapter books have 40 to 60 pages • Simple narrative nonfiction • Some simple biography • Some persuasive text • Characteristics of genre are evident and support predictions • Illustrations include some key details about text • Some unusual formats, such as letters or questions followed by answers • **Texts of eight to 16 pages** • Nonfiction text includes text features and simple graphics • **Easy chapter books have 40 to 60 pages** • Smaller print • Some longer (10 words or more) and more complex sentences • **Sentences may carry over to two or three lines, and some over two pages** • Text features and structures may support predictions
Linguistic Systems	• **Longer sentences** • Texts include three- to four-syllable words • Texts include common compound words • Texts include words with common prefixes and suffixes • Texts include words with complex spelling patterns, multisyllabic words, and words with inflectional endings, plurals, contractions, and possessive

Developing Reader 3 (DR3)

Meaning-Making Systems	• Frequently occurring roots and affixes • Text includes words that help the reader visualize • Stories include central message or lesson • **Main character(s) in fiction text demonstrate traits through their actions** • **Story may be told by different characters/narrators at various points in a text** • Text includes text features that support predictions • Persuasive text makes it clear what the author is trying to persuade the reader to think or do

Developing Reader 4 (DR4)

Surface Systems	• Slightly more complex informational texts • Slightly more complex genres (e.g., some biographies of familiar people) • Images and illustrations help to clarify text and support comprehension • Text features in nonfiction text provide information that connects to main text • **Beginning chapter books with supporting illustrations** • Informational text may include a glossary • **Forty to 75 pages** • **Many lines of print on a page**
Linguistic Systems	• **Varied placement of subject, verb, adjectives, and adverbs in sentences** • **Increasingly more complex sentences** • Texts with complex spelling patterns, multisyllabic words, and words with inflectional endings, plurals, contractions, and possessives
Meaning-Making Systems	• Some bolded words to indicate key words • Some compound words (por ejemplo: pasar, pasatiempo; sacar, sacapuntas, bien, bienvenidos) • Book's central message or lesson is clearly based on the story's events • **Connections are made between and among historical events, scientific ideas or concepts, or steps in technical procedures in a nonfiction text** • **Some traits or feelings of the main character may not be obvious** • Story may be told by different characters/narrators at various points in a text

Developing Reader 5 (DR5)	
Surface Systems	• Informational texts that include historical facts, scientific ideas, or technical procedures • Informational text that is persuasive • More complex genres (e.g., fables, drama) • Poetry with visual patterns • Images and illustrations help to clarify text and support comprehension • Beginning chapter books • Informational texts include various text features (e.g., captions, bold print, subheadings, glossaries, indexes, electronic menus, icons) • Print and graphic features are used to achieve specific purposes • Varied organization in nonfiction text formats (question/answer, boxes, legends, etc.) • Nonfiction text includes organization and resources to look for information (e.g., title, table of contents) • **Sixty to 100 pages of print** • Some fiction text has a great deal of dialogue within a story
Linguistic Systems	**N/A**
Meaning-Making Systems	• Frequently occurring affixes added to lesser-known words (por ejemplo: feliz-infeliz, contar-recontar) • Words and phrases that are used to create rhythm and meaning in a story or poem • May include affixes, including re-, pre-, -ción, and ísimo/ísima, to determine the meaning of words and subsequently use the newly acquired words • Inclusion of antonyms, synonyms, idioms, and homographs in context • May include homographs, homophones, and commonly confused terms such as porque/porqué/por qué/por que, sino/si no, and también/tan bien • Text features, characteristics of genre, and structures support predictions • Fiction text includes explicit characteristics and structures such as the central idea and supporting evidence • **Nonfiction text includes clear organizational patterns such as chronological order and cause and effect** • Characters in a story respond to major events and challenges • **Characters interact in ways that convey information about their characteristics** • **Characters' different points of view are depicted**

Table 5.5: Text Characteristics of Transitioning Reader Levels

Transitioning Reader Exemplars

La Escapada de Ema by Angelica Dossetti
Soñadores by Yuyi Morales
Inventoras y sus inventos by Aitziber Lopez and Luciano Lozano
Secretos para convertirse en científico by Sang-wook Yi

	Transitioning Reader 1 (TR1)
Surface Systems	• Poetry uses rhyme scheme, meter, and graphical elements of all types such as punctuation and capitalization in poems across a variety of poetic forms • Images or illustrations are used to contribute to what is conveyed in words • **Chapter books** • Nonfiction may include organizational patterns such as compare and contrast
Linguistic Systems	• **Longer (more than 15 words) and more complex sentences**
Meaning-Making Systems	• **One to two academic vocabulary words/phrases per page** • Frequently occurring affixes added to lesser-known words (por ejemplo: feliz-infeliz, contar-recontar) • Words and phrases that are used to create rhythm and meaning in a story or poem • Stories include a central message, lesson, or moral • **Traits and actions of characters in a story contribute to the sequence of events** • **Strong relationships between and among historical events, scientific ideas or concepts, or steps in technical procedures in a nonfiction text are conveyed through language that pertains to time, sequence, and cause/effect**
	Transitioning Reader 2 (TR2)
Surface Systems	• Most genres including dramas, poetry, or myths • Narratives have more elaborate plots • Images or illustrations are used to contribute to what is conveyed in words • **Fiction may be based on concepts that are distant in time and space and reflect diverse cultures** • Informational texts include text features and search tools • **Variety of structures in informational text (e.g., chronology, comparison, cause/effect, problem/solution)** • **Sixty to 100 pages of print**
Linguistic Systems	**N/A**

Meaning-Making Systems	• One to two academic vocabulary words/phrases per page
	• Words and phrases with literal and nonliteral meanings (por ejemplo: Tomar medidas. Está lloviendo a cántaros)
	• Real-life connection between words and their use (por ejemplo: describen a personas. Que son simpáticas o serviciales)
	• Text includes descriptive words, some complex content-specific words, and some technical words
	• **Words that have shades of meaning that describe states of mind or degrees of certainty and the use of the subjunctive mode to express doubt**
	• Nonfiction texts include underlying organizational structures (description, compare and contrast, problem and solution, cause and effect)
	• **Stories include subtle ideas**
	• Literary and nonfiction text include a theme or central idea that emerges, shaped and refined through specific details over the course of the text
	• Plot elements, including the use of foreshadowing and suspense, may be used to advance the plot
	• Setting may influence character and plot development
	• Rhetorical devices such as direct address and rhetorical questions and logical fallacies such as loaded language and sweeping generalizations may be used
	• **Narrative nonfiction may include both fact and opinion**
	• **Expository text may include both fact and opinion**

Table 5.6: Text Characteristics of Developing Independence Reader Levels

Developing Independence Reader Exemplars

Yacay en las tierras del buen viento by Luz María del Valle
Una cabeza distinta by Luis Panini
¿Y si . . . ? by David J. Smith

	Developing Independence Reader 1 (DIR1)
Surface Systems	• Genres include biographies of lesser-known people, humor, historical fiction, collections of short stories, and science fiction
	• **Minimal illustrations in literary text; most of the content carried by print rather than pictures**
	• **More difficult layout of informational text, and some fiction text, with denser format**
Linguistic Systems	• **Some lengthy, complex sentences containing prepositional phrases, introductory clauses, and lists of nouns, verbs, or adjectives**

Developing Independence Reader 1 (DIR1)

Meaning-Making Systems	• Words with prefixes and suffixes • Three to five academic vocabulary words/phrases per page • May include figures of speech • Language may include imagery, literal and figurative language such as simile and metaphor, and sound devices such as alliteration and assonance to achieve specific purposes • General academic and domain-specific words and phrases, including those that signal precise actions, emotions, or states of being (por ejemplo: emocionado, afligido, eufórico) and that are basic to a particular topic (ejemplo: vida silvestre, conservación y en peligro de extinción cuando se habla de la protección de los animales) • Story, drama, or poem includes a theme • **Story may include multiple causes and effects** • In-depth characters with both good and bad traits who change and develop over time • **Points of view of the narrators or characters are clearly conveyed** • **Author's point of view or purpose in a nonfiction text is clearly conveyed**

Developing Independence Reader 2 (DIR2)

Surface Systems	• Increasingly varied genres such as fiction with elaborate plots, legends, hybrids, and myths • Nonfiction genres include argumentative text • Variety of structures in informational text (e.g., chronology, comparison, cause/effect, problem/solution) • Minimal illustrations in literary text; most of the content carried by print rather than pictures • Nonfiction text includes features that support understanding such as sections, tables, graphs, time lines, bullets, numbers, and bold and italicized font • Nonfiction may contain a variety of complex graphics, often more than one on a page
Linguistic Systems	• **Longer (more than 15 words) and more complex sentences** • May include palabras agudas, graves, esdrújulas, and sobresdrújulas (words with the stress on the last, penultimate, and antepenultimate syllable and words with the stress on the syllable before the antepenultimate)
Meaning-Making Systems	• **Many complex content-specific words in nonfiction, mostly defined in text, illustrations, or glossary** • Some use of Greek and Latin roots • Common Greek and Latin affixes (por ejemplo: telégrafo, fotografía, autógrafo) • Simple similes and metaphors (por ejemplo: tan bonito como una fotografía) • Common idioms, adages, and proverbs • General academic and domain-specific words and phrases (por ejemplo: emocionado, afligido, eufórico)

- Words and phrases that are basic to a particular topic (por ejemplo: vida silvestre, conservación y en peligro de extinción cuando se habla de la protección de los animales)
- Some words and phrases that allude to significant characters found in mythology (por ejemplo: Hércules)
- May include words with affixes, such as mono-, sobre-, sub-, inter-, poli-, -able, -ante, -eza, -ancia, and -ura; and roots, including auto, bio, grafía, metro, fono, and tele
- May include idioms, homographs, and homophones such as abrasar/abrazar
- May include homographs, homophones, and commonly confused terms such as porque/porqué/por qué/por que, sino/si no, and también/tan bien
- May include a story, drama, or poem with a theme
- May include anecdotes
- **Specific information is used to explain events, procedures, ideas, or concepts in a historical, scientific, or technical text**

Table 5.7: Text Characteristics of Independent Reader Levels

Independent Reader Exemplars

Otelo by Sara Bertrand
¿Por qué peleamos? by Niki Walker
Cuentos Mayas by Judy Goldman

Independent Reader 1 (IR1)	
Surface Systems	• Increasingly varied genres such as tall tales, folktales • More complex narrative structures (e.g., story-within-a story, flashback) • Informational text includes elements such as the controlling idea or thesis with supporting evidence; features such as introduction, foreword, preface, references, or acknowledgments to gain background information; and organizational patterns such as definition, classification, advantage, and disadvantage • Minimal illustrations in literary text; most of the content carried by print rather than pictures • Increasingly difficult layout of informational texts, with dense content and format
Linguistic Systems	• Wide range of declarative, imperative, or interrogative sentences
Meaning-Making Systems	• Three to five general academic or domain-specific vocabulary words/phrases per page • Many words with affixes (prefixes and suffixes) • Simple similes and metaphors (por ejemplo: tan bonito como una fotografía) • Some idioms, adages, and proverbs • Context provides clues to indicate meaning of words or phrases (e.g., cause/effect relationships and comparisons in text)

Independent Reader 1 (IR1)

- Story, drama, or poem includes a theme that is conveyed through particular details
- Characters interact in ways that convey information about their characteristics
- Nonfiction text is made more complex through the relationships or interactions between and among two or more individuals, events, ideas, or concepts in a historical, scientific, or technical text
- Characters in plays are developed through dialogue and staging
- Points of view of the narrators or characters are well developed
- Author's point of view or purpose in a nonfiction text is clearly conveyed

Independent Reader 2 (IR2)

Surface Systems	• More complex genres • Specific types of poetry (sonnet, soliloquy) • Some poetry uses sound devices and figurative language in a variety of poetic forms • Drama includes structures such as character tags, acts, scenes, and stage directions • Informational text includes structures such as the central idea with supporting evidence; features such as insets, time lines, and sidebars to support understanding; and organizational patterns such as logical order and order of importance • Most fiction texts with minimal illustrations or no illustrations other than the cover
Linguistic Systems	N/A
Meaning-Making Systems	• **Six to 10 academic vocabulary words/phrases per page** • Words used in regional or historical dialects; some words from languages other than Spanish • Many words with affixes (prefixes and suffixes) • **The position or function in a sentence provides clues to the meaning of some words** • Relationship between particular words provides clues to the meaning of each of the words (por ejemplo: relaciones de causa/efecto, parte/todo, elemento/categoría) • Words and phrases with figurative, connotative, and technical meanings • Literary works may include rhymes and other repetitions of sounds (e.g., alliteration) that contribute to meaning • Text may include words with affixes, such as trans-, super-, anti-, semi-, -logía, -ificar, -ismo, and -ista; and roots, including audi, crono, foto, geo, and terr • Text may include idioms, adages, and puns • Text may include homographs, homophones, and commonly confused terms such as porque/porqué/por qué/por que, sino/si no, and también/tan bien • Includes palabras agudas, graves, esdrújulas, and sobresdrújulas (words with the stress on the last, penultimate, and antepenultimate syllable and words with the stress on the syllable before the antepenultimate)

- Language such as hyperbole, stereotyping, and anecdote may contribute to the text's voice
- **Literary text includes a theme or central idea developed over the course of the text and conveyed through particular details**
- Nonfiction text has two or more central ideas developed over the course of the text
- The plot of literary text unfolds in a series of episodes and includes characters who respond or change as the plot moves toward a resolution
- Key individuals, events, or ideas are introduced, illustrated, or elaborated upon in a variety of ways (e.g., through examples or anecdotes)
- Elements of a story or drama interact (e.g., setting shapes the characters or plot)
- **Nonfiction text includes interactions between individuals, events, and ideas in a text (e.g., how ideas influence individuals or events, or how individuals influence ideas or events)**
- Points of view of the narrators or characters are well developed and contrast with one another
- Author's point of view or purpose in a nonfiction text is clearly conveyed, and the author's position is distinguished from those of others

Independent Reader 3 (IR3)

Surface Systems	• Expanding types of complex genres • A wide variety of complex graphics that require interpretation (photos with legends, diagrams, labels, cutaways, graphics, maps)
Linguistic Systems	N/A
Meaning-Making Systems	• **Long, multisyllabic words requiring attention to roots to read and understand** • May include analogies or allusions to other texts • Figurative language such as metaphor and personification used to achieve a specific purpose • **Literary devices may include omniscient and limited point of view** • Author's use of language contributes to mood and voice • May use rhetorical devices and logical fallacies • May determine the meaning and usage of grade-level academic Spanish words derived from Greek and Latin roots, including metro-, grafo-, scrib-, and port- • Text may differentiate between and use homographs, homophones, and commonly confused terms such as porque/porqué/por qué/por que, sino/si no, and también/tan bien • Literary text includes a theme or central idea developed over the course of the text and conveyed through particular details • **Nonfiction text has two or more central ideas developed over the course of the text** • Particular lines of dialogue or incidents in a story or drama propel the action, reveal aspects of a character, or provoke a decision

	Independent Reader 3 (IR3)

- Nonfiction text makes connections among and distinctions between individuals, ideas, or events (e.g., through comparisons, analogies, or categories)
- **Differences in the points of view of the characters and the audience or reader (e.g., created through the use of dramatic irony) create such effects as suspense or humor**
- **Author's point of view or purpose in a text is explicitly acknowledged, and author responds to conflicting evidence or viewpoints**

	Independent Reader 4 (IR4)

Surface Systems	• Expanding types of complex genres including satire, epic, and ballad • Poetry uses rhyme scheme, meter, and graphical elements of all types such as punctuation and capitalization in poems across a variety of poetic forms • Informational text includes characteristics and structural elements including the controlling idea or thesis with supporting evidence; features such as references or acknowledgments, chapters, sections, subsections, bibliography, tables, graphs, captions, bullets, and numbers; and organizational patterns that support multiple topics, categories, and subcategories • **Unusual text organizations (e.g., flashbacks)**
Linguistic Systems	• **Some very long sentences (more than 30 words)**
Meaning-Making Systems	• **Eleven to 15 academic vocabulary words/phrases per page** • Words that are archaic, come from regional dialect, or from languages other than Spanish • Sophisticated use of figures of speech (e.g., euphemism, oxymoron) • Words and phrases are used in the text to create a cumulative impact on meaning and tone (e.g., how the language sets a sense of time and place; how it sets a formal or informal tone; how the language of a court opinion differs from that of a newspaper) • Literary and nonfiction text includes a theme or central idea that emerges, shaped and refined through specific details over the course of the text • Plot elements, including the use of foreshadowing and suspense, may be used to advance the plot • Setting may influence character and plot development • Rhetorical devices, such as direct address; and rhetorical questions and logical fallacies, such as loaded language and sweeping generalizations, may be used • **Complex characters (e.g., those with multiple or conflicting motivations) develop over the course of a text, interact with other characters, and advance the plot or develop the theme** • **Characters' qualities may influence events and resolution of the conflict** • **Authors use rhetoric to advance their point of view or purpose in a nonfiction text**

Independent Reader 5 (IR5)

Surface Systems	• All genres • Informational text includes characteristics and structural elements such as the controlling idea or thesis with supporting evidence; features such as footnotes, endnotes, and citations; and multiple organizational patterns within a text to develop the thesis • **Books with variation in color to communicate mood (e.g., sepia, black and-white, color)** • May use graphical elements such as punctuation and line length in poems across a variety of poetic forms such as epic, lyric, and humorous poetry
Linguistic Systems	N/A
Meaning-Making Systems	• **Sixteen to 21+ academic vocabulary words/phrases per page** • Words and phrases with figurative and connotative meanings that impact meaning and tone, including words with multiple meanings or language that is particularly fresh, engaging, or beautiful (Incluir a Cervantes, así como a otros autores de lengua española) • May use context within or beyond a paragraph to clarify the meaning of unfamiliar or ambiguous words • May use words that name actions, directions, positions, sequences, and locations • May use multiple-meaning words, homographs, homophones, and commonly confused terms correctly • May include words and phrases with figurative, connotative, and technical meanings that are used to refine the meaning of a key term or terms over the course of a text (por ejemplo: cómo define Bolívar "país" y "patria" en La carta de Jamaica) • **Literary and nonfiction text includes two or more themes or central ideas that interact and build on one another over the course of the text** • **Stories may include nonlinear plot development such as flashbacks, foreshadowing, subplots, and parallel plot structures** • Dramatic action is developed through the use of acts and scenes in plays • May use literary devices including multiple points of view and irony • May use language to contribute to the mood, voice, and tone • **May use rhetorical devices, such as analogy and juxtaposition; and logical fallacies, such as bandwagon appeals and circular reasoning** • Text includes a complex set of ideas or sequence of events that develop over the course of the text • **Author conveys point of view in ways that require the reader to distinguish what is directly stated in a text from what is meant (e.g., satire, sarcasm, irony, or understatement)** • Author's point of view or purpose in a text is conveyed through rhetoric that is particularly effective in which style and content contribute to the power, persuasiveness, or beauty of the text

Chapter 6

Leveled Books in the Classroom

The literacies of Latinx students are not static and are never monolingual, even when the text is one language or another. There are no monolingual texts if bilingual children are engaged in reading.

—Ofelia Garcia

KEY POINTS IN CHAPTER 6

- The key to matching readers with appropriate leveled text is to consider the instructional purpose.
- The greatest gains in literacy are made when students have ample time to read and write.
- The most valid assessment of reading comes from the teachers' informal observations on a day-to-day basis.

INSTRUCTIONAL STRUCTURES AND DESIGN

Although the primary purpose of this chapter is to help the reader understand how to implement leveled text in the classroom, the importance of integrated units as a part of dual-language curriculum design must be addressed before going into the details of teaching students to read Spanish.

Integrated units are units of study that incorporate science and social studies content with ELA standards and are guided by universal concepts and compelling questions (Dove, Honigsfeld, & Cohan, 2014). Amy Mosquera has contributed a piece on "The Power of a Paired Curricular Framework" (see appendix D) that explains designing units that include reading and writing instruction through the content areas.

In our experience, when teachers are introduced to new instructional systems or programs, they usually want to know, "What does that look like in the classroom?" This chapter attempts to answer that question by first providing a possible breakdown of the reading block and the instructional structures within the reading block. Then the chapter will dive deeper into each instructional structure and how to teach the components of the Reading Tapestry within those structures.

Finally, chapter 6 will connect the information provided in previous chapters and explain how to match the leveled text with the readers, how to use the leveled text in the classroom, and how to provide ongoing assessment to adjust the levels of text used with readers as they grow and develop.

The Reading Block

It is recommended that all students engage in a minimum of 90 minutes of daily reading instruction (additional time for daily writing instruction is included in the literacy block). Although specific schedules will vary, table 6.1 shows an example of a 90-minute daily reading block. This block is the structure in which the instructional design and components of the Reading Tapestry are applied.

Fisher and Frey (2008) determined that four basic instructional moves promote learning: focus lesson, guided instruction, collaborative work, and independent work. Basic instructional design includes a systematic gradual release of responsibility beginning with the teacher providing direct instruction and modeling during a focus lesson provided to the whole group.

The teacher then provides opportunities for the students to apply what was taught to the whole group through guided instruction. During guided instruction, the teacher carefully observes and assesses the students' proficiency with applying the newly learned skills and strategies. When the teacher becomes confident that the students are ready to work together, the next step is to give a collaborative task or assignment.

During a reading block, the collaborative task is often a brief turn and talk during the whole-group instruction, or a collaborative task to complete while the teacher is meeting with small groups. As responsibility shifts entirely to the students, they are given independent work or asked to confer with the teacher to demonstrate their individual proficiency at the skill or strategy.

Reading Block

Timing Minutes 90-Minute Block	K–2	Timing Minutes 90-Minute Block	3–5
10–20	**Whole-Group Focus Lesson:** **Language Comprehension**	10–20	**Whole-Group Focus Lesson:** **Language Comprehension**
35–45	**Independent Literacy Work Time** **Teacher** — **Students** *Teacher:* Independent Reading Conferences Small-Group Instruction: • Guided Reading • Strategy Lessons *Students:* Independent Reading Independent or Collaborative Literacy Tasks Small-Group Instruction: • Guided Reading • Strategy Lesson	40–50	**Independent Literacy Work Time** **Teacher** — **Students** *Teacher:* Independent Reading Conferences Small-Group Instruction: • Guided Reading • Strategy Lessons • Book Clubs *Students:* Independent Reading Independent or Collaborative Literacy Tasks Small-Group Instruction: • Guided Reading • Strategy Lessons • Book Clubs
5 10–20	**Whole-Group Share/Check-In** **Whole Group:** *Word Recognition and Language Structures* Systematic Instruction in Phonemic and Phonological Awareness, Oracy, Decoding, High-Frequency Words, Cross-Linguistic Connections, Translanguaging	5 10–20	**Whole-Group Share/Check-In** **Whole Group:** *Word Recognition and Language Structures* Systematic Instruction in Decoding, Cross-Linguistic Connections, Translanguaging

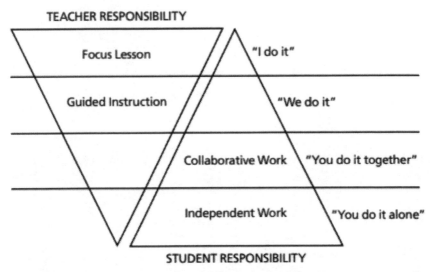

Figure 6.1. Gradual Release of Responsibility (Fisher and Frey, 2008). "Better Learning through Structured Teaching: A Framework for the Gradual Release of Responsibility," by Douglas Fisher and Nancy Frey, Alexandria, VA: ASCD. Copyright 2008 by ASCD.

Stages of Reader Development and Text Levels of Text in the Reading Block

As discussed in detail in chapter 3, most children follow a pattern of reading behaviors as they learn to read. Understanding and being able to identify the seven stages of reader development give teachers a framework of skills that can be observed, taught, and supported as their students become increasingly proficient readers. Table 6.2 shows the alignment of the stage of gradual

Table 6.2

Gradual Release	Instructional Structure	System to Help Guide Text Selection
"I Do It"	Whole Group: Focus Lesson	Stage of Reader Development
"We Do It"	Small Group: Strategy Skill Group	Leveling Instrument/Stage of Reader Development
"We Do It"	Small Group: Guided Reading	Leveling Instrument
"You Do It Together"	Collaborative Literacy Tasks	Leveling Instrument/Stage of Reader Development
"You Do It Alone"	Individual: Conferring	Leveling Instrument
"You Do It Alone"	Individual: Independent Reading	Stage of Reader Development

release, the instructional structures in the reading block, and the DCC lectura system that will guide text selection for instruction.

When planning instructional structures that are broader in scope (i.e., whole-group and collaborative tasks) or purpose (i.e., independent reading), it is best to select books within the entire range of the stage of reader development. When planning instructional structures that are designed for specific skills (i.e., guided reading, strategy skill group) or students (i.e., conferring), it is best to select leveled books that are a good match for the student(s). A chart that shows how the DCC lectura stages of reader development and text levels align with other leveling systems can be found at www .readingtapestry.com.

INSTRUCTIONAL STRUCTURES

Whole Group is the broadest level of instruction; its purpose is to provide all students with exposure to grade-level standards regardless of their reading proficiency. To maintain the rigor of the instruction that students receive, it is crucial that all students are exposed to grade-level standards and to text that is appropriate for the stage of reading development that aligns with the grade level in which instruction is occurring.

Small-Group instruction includes two basic structures: guided reading and strategy/skill group. Students who are gathered together in a strategy skill group have been identified to have a common goal that they need to work on. The goal will determine whether it is best that the text be at the specific level for the student (not all students need to be reading the same level of text to work on the same strategy/skill goal) or it is sufficient to work on text simply at the students' stage of reading development.

In guided reading, students will be grouped together with other students who would benefit from reading the same leveled text. Guided reading groups are most effective when the students are provided direct instruction on specific skills and strategies of particular significance at that level of text (see chapter 5 for the bolded characteristics at each level).

As an example of providing direct instruction, if a group of students have been successful reading books at the TR1 level, the teacher may select a nonfiction book at the TR2 level and provide direct instruction on the structures of the information text because that is a bolded characteristic at that level. Providing targeted and systematic instruction about the characteristics of the next level of text will give the students the leverage they need to navigate the text successfully.

Collaborative Literacy is not only during brief turn and talks or pair sharing. At times teachers may choose to give students collaborative literacy tasks to be done while she meets with other students in small groups. Students could work collaboratively in an unlimited number of ways on tasks that relate to the day's focus lesson. For example, students may partner-read, do word work, engage in discussion during book club, or play a game of "heads up" to practice vocabulary words.

Conferring is used both as an assessment structure and for brief points of instruction. The text being used during conferences depends on the student's needs. If a student has been working on specific, skill-based goals within the linguistic systems, a text that reflects the specific level at which that individual is working is likely to be the most beneficial. If the instructional goal is within the meaning-making systems, text that aligns with the student's stage of reading development will be the best fit.

Independent Reading plays a crucial role in the development of readers. A vast amount of research confirms that the greatest gains in literacy are made when students have ample time to read and write. The American Library Association (2010) statement on the value of independent reading provides guidelines for encouraging students to value and enjoy reading. Their suggestions include providing students with

- access to current, quality, and high-interest books;
- time during the school day dedicated to reading for pleasure; and
- school environments in which independent reading is valued.

Engaging students in reading high-interest books is the priority during independent reading. Students may not select books to read independently that are at their instructional level, or even within their stage of development. The primary goal of independent reading time is to have the opportunity to self-select books and to have plenty of time to become engaged with quality books to apply learned skills and to experience the joy of reading.

MATCHING READERS WITH LEVELED TEXT

Once a student's current stage of reader development has been determined, the key to matching readers with appropriate leveled text is to consider the instructional purpose. Teachers can determine the instructional purpose by answering the following questions:

1. Which skills are the most crucial for the students to learn?
2. In what order should those skills be taught?
3. What are the best instructional structures to teach the skills?

Which skills are most crucial?

- Refer to the DCC lectura method's progression of skills (see chapter 2).
- Find the students' stages of reader development (refer to "Reader Characteristics by Level" at www.readingtapestry.com).
  - Which skills is the student demonstrating successfully and are a strength for the reader?
  - Which skills are holding the student back from being successful at the next level of text?

In what order should the skills be taught?

- Refer to the DCC lectura method's progression of skills (see chapter 2).
- Consider the general progression of skills to be taught within a given level of text based on the Spanish Reading Tapestry:
  - literacy knowledge
  - oracy
  - phonemic and phonological awareness
  - decoding
  - fluency
  - language structures
  - vocabulary
  - Comprehension
- Refer to the reader characteristics by level at www.readingtapestry.com and consider which skills the student is not yet applying proficiently.

Which is the best structure to teach the skills?

- Consider which instructional structures are best to teach the identified strategy/skill.
- Table 6.1 shows how each of these instructional structures can be supported by stage of reader development, text level, or both and is followed by a description of each instructional structure.

Looking at How to Match Leveled Text to Readers through Case Studies

To put it all together, consider the following case studies and how the process described so far in this chapter is used to match readers to leveled text.

Case Study #1: Nick

Nick is a kindergarten student whose teacher used the quick check to determine that his reader stage of development is emergent reader. The first step was to consider which reading behaviors were Nick's strengths and which were areas for growth.

Nick's teacher knows that he has been exposed to many types of text and can describe the relationship between illustrations and words in the text. Nick's teacher has noticed that he decodes words with silent h and consonant digraphs, but he has difficulty decoding some common two-syllable words. While reading ER3 level text, Nick is monitoring his reading and attempts to self-correct decoding errors, but he reads word by word and with no expression. Table 6.3 lists the observed strengths as well as the areas for growth and the instructional structures most appropriate to address the need.

It is unlikely that Nick will be able to read ER3 level text fluently until he has increased skill with syllable structures. It is developmentally appropriate to address the phonics needs first, so his teacher should provide direct instruction on the CVCV skill during a strategy group with other students who also need to work on the same skill.

Once he successfully demonstrates the ability to decode all common syllable structures, his teacher can shift the focus to building fluency, first through phrasing and expression. When working on fluency, his teacher may want to drop the text level to an ER2 for a brief time so Nick can apply as he is learning about fluency to text that is easier for him to navigate and with which he will feel more confident. As his fluency and confidence increase, Nick's teacher can work with him on comprehension in guided reading at levels ER3 and ER4 (depending on his familiarity with the content).

Table 6.3

Strengths:
• Consistently monitoring reading and attempting to self-correct
• Recognizes common types of texts (e.g., storybooks, poems)
• Decodes words with silent h and consonant digraphs such as /ch/, /rr/, and /ll/

Areas for Growth:	Instructional Structures:
• Not familiar with all syllable structures • Unable to decode common two-syllable words with any syllable combination • Struggling to recognize that new words are created when syllables are changed, added, or deleted	• Direct instruction on syllable structures and combinations
• Phrasing is off or, at times, reading word by word • Inconsistent use of expression when reading	• Build fluency during guided reading group using ER2 level text and building toward the ability to read ER3 level text fluently

Case Study #2: Olivia

Olivia is a second-grade student whose teacher used the quick check to determine that her reader stage of development is beginning reader. Olivia demonstrates the ability to successfully decode BR1 level text with automaticity and to demonstrate understanding of a fiction story by retelling it with minimal support.

Based on the description of the beginning reader stage of development, key interactions with text at the beginning reader stage of development relate to reading without finger pointing and recognizing high-frequency words by sight. Yet, Olivia reads haltingly, stumbling over high-frequency words that are on the emergent reader list. She uses word-by-word finger pointing and frequently relies on decoding every word, even those familiar to her.

The first step is to consider which reading behaviors are Olivia's strengths and which are areas for growth for her. Olivia's teacher has observed Olivia reading a BR1 level book and noticed the behaviors listed on table 6.4.

Although Olivia clearly has successful decoding skills at the BR stage of development, Olivia is not applying the skills with automaticity. To read a level BR1 successfully, she will need to build her fluency. It is developmentally appropriate for her to work on fluency skills at a level of text lower than she is able to decode. The teacher should provide direct fluency instruction with a level ER3 text to build Olivia's confidence and fluency.

As her fluency improves, Olivia can progress to a level ER4 and then to an BR1. Olivia shows strong comprehension at the ER levels, but once at BR1

Table 6.4

Strengths:

- Enjoys reading and has favorite books
- Strong concept of return sweep
- Strong and automatic decoding
- Recognizes some high-frequency words in isolation
- Makes connections to personal experiences, ideas in other texts, and society with adult assistance

Areas for Growth:	Instructional Structures:
• Build fluency by increase practice of tracking print with eyes • Continued practice of reading high-frequency words in text • Encourage voice-print match that is smooth and automatic • Practice oral reading that demonstrates phrasing and appropriate stress on words	• Build fluency during small-group instruction using ER3 level text and building toward the ability to read BR1 level text fluently

the teacher should take care to ensure that Olivia demonstrates story understandings through artwork, retellings, and role play with guidance before
attempting to instruct her using BR2 level of text.

Focusing on the reading behaviors holding Olivia back from being successful will involve encouraging her to read silently for increasingly longer
periods of time and to understand the importance of reading fluency. The best
instructional structure to teach these skills is to focus on the fluency during
small-group instruction that provides lots of instructional support as she navi-
gates toward the more demanding BR1 level text.

In addition, she should work on increasing reading stamina during independent reading time using books that she self-selects among the full range
of ER stage of development. This example demonstrates how multiple levels
of text can be appropriate for the same student depending on the instructional purpose.

HOW ARE LEVELED TEXT USED
TO DEVELOP READERS?

How to Advance Students' Stages of
Reader Development

The DCC lectura method promotes the employment of diagnostic teaching,
whereby the teacher observes the student's progress during instruction and
creates an individualized path for learning. As teachers work with students
in whole group, small groups, and while conferring with individuals, they
should use ongoing assessment to determine the students' current range of
skills and how they are advancing in their stages of reader development.

In this process, the line between teaching and assessing is blurry to the
point of almost being indistinguishable. For reading teachers, assessment is
an essential daily activity. As Fountas and Pinnell (1996) state, "the primary
purpose of assessment is to gather data to inform teaching. If assessment does
not result in improved teaching, then its value in school diminishes greatly."

As teachers do whole-group instruction, their eyes are scanning the room,
checking for engagement and understanding. While the teacher meets with
small groups, students are listening to other students whisper read and making note of the reading behaviors they observe. During a reading conference,
the teacher is listening to a student discuss his comprehension of the text,
gauging the level to which he comprehended the text, and deciding on teaching points for the conference. Teachers' day-to-day informal and ongoing
assessment serves a multitude of purposes including

- tracking students' growth and ability to navigate a given level of text;
- informing teaching decisions;
- assessing the students' skills and ability to tackle the next level of text;
- finding out what the child can do, both independently and with teacher support;
- documenting progress for parents and students; and
- reporting to administrators, MTSS teams, PLCs, and teams focusing on problem solving.

A variety of systems can be put in place to track students' growth as teachers informally assess during instruction. One way would be to download the reader characteristics by level tables found at www.readingtapestry.com. The tables can be used as a guide to assess how the students are progressing through the characteristics at a given level and their potential to navigate text at increasingly challenging levels.

Additional Metrics of Success

Although our firm belief is that the most valid assessment of reading is the informal observations that teachers do on a day-to-day basis, at times teachers may want the assurance that a more formal assessment affords before advancing a student's level of instructional text or before meeting with a parent. At those times, the teacher may choose to give the formative assessment of reader (FARC).

Characteristics of the FARC are found on our website, www.readingtapestry .com. FARC is a tool that helps teachers observe and record the reader characteristics of students as they read and discuss leveled text. By using the FARC, teachers will be able to monitor their students' developmental progress to ensure that the leveled text being matched with the reader is the most appropriate instructional level.

One final measure provided at www.readingtapestry.com is the quick check of fluency rubric. It is a guide to assess a student's oral reading fluency of leveled text. It is recommended that teachers download and copy the reproducible rubric and refer to it while working with students who have been identified with a fluency skill deficit.

Appendix A

Effective Advocates: The Missing Link between Home and School Cultures

Geri Chaffee

Advocacy usually starts with a question. Mine is, why do children learning English as a second language do so poorly in K–12 schools? The passion that effective advocates require stems from the moral indignation at something not being quite right. If you are reading this book, you have worked with students who most likely are marginalized because they are part of a minority culture or may speak a second language. Perhaps you, too, share similar educational experiences and can appreciate the promise and potential of these students; perhaps that is why you choose to be a teacher.

Teaching a profession often lends itself to working in silos. We spend most of our time in our classroom with our students, desperately trying to get through all the material they are supposed to learn in one year and all the additional duties required of us. We have little time to keep up with policy and practice of the district, the state, much less the nation when it comes to education and the social forces that affect our students directly. There is, however, plenty of interest in the advocacy of dual-language education programs, because all students do better academically across all content areas when they learn in two languages. As a result, dual-language immersion and ELL educators are in a unique position to change hearts and minds. Our mission is to improve the lives of children and families through education and end the cycle of remediation and despair.

English learners (ELs) have become the fastest growing student population in the country; yet US schools were never designed to teach students who do not understand English. School districts are faced with the realization that

they have to adapt their instructional methods to address the education, accul-
turation, and socio-emotional needs of these students so that, at a minimum.
As bilingual educators, we all have experienced the pervasive attitudes that
consistently "otherize" entire student populations. Effective advocates must
build bridges and understanding even when confronted with language and
actions that are discriminatory. The best way to do this is by asking questions, listening, and knowing the facts. It takes patience, facts, and figures to
influence, and we must realize that at any given time, we may know more
about dual-language education and its astounding impact on students than the
leaders we are trying to persuade.

We can use many tactics, depending on our comfort level, to expedite the
path to advocacy. First, know your data and speak with confidence about the
important work we are doing in promoting bilingualism in all our students.
Other ways to develop different levels of school and community support are:

1. Bring our Hispanic families into the school culture with consistent communication and support services.
2. Develop Spanish-speaking leaders from your parent pool and local
   organizations.
3. Identify potential allies to support dual-language programs.
4. Identify community organizations that could benefit Hispanic families
   and offer to translate or help with outreach.
5. Connect people, products, and services.
6. Help schools develop a list of local resources for parents and families.
7. Identify influencers in your community and state and keep them
   apprised of student success stories.
8. Involve nonprofit foundations, philanthropy, and local churches.
9. Increase communication within social media networks in both English
   and Spanish.
10. Develop relationships with local print and broadcast news media.

We as educators have within us the knowledge, the talent, and the passion to become effective advocates, and we must incorporate advocacy as a
natural part of our personal and professional lives. This is the only way that
our impact will be maximized to positively affect our students. We must find
a way to interject narratives that not only humanize the families we seek to
impact, but also dispel the stereotypes. It helps to have specific examples
about success in other schools and districts that can connect with our listener
at the right moment, whether it's one person, a small informal group, or a
large audience.

At all times, your smile and joy will be infectious and make others want
to be a part of these initiatives—because they truly change lives. Helping

children develop into happy, healthy, self-sufficient, bilingual adults who can not only retain a connection with their language and culture but also enrich our nation as a whole is well worth the effort.

Appendix B

Additive Approach to Multilingualism

Dr. Kris Nicholls

In the United States, the most common approach taken with students who arrive at the schoolroom door speaking a language other than English is to immerse them in English-only instruction, heralding the call of Theodore Roosevelt for all to come together in the proverbial "melting pot." In this analogy, which assumes that all persons whose home language is other than English want to become "true Americans" and be monolingual speakers of English, these students must give up their home language and culture to "blend in" among other Americans (Smith, 2012). This approach is considered "subtractive," requiring that the home language and culture be extinguished, and English become the sole language of the student.

In the decades since Roosevelt's pronouncement, English-only instruction for these students has become the default policy in American schools. Students whose home language is other than English are seen through a deficit lens, labeled "non-English proficient" or "limited English-proficient." Even the current labels of "English learner" or "English language learner" highlight that the student has not yet learned English. A new term has emerged, "emergent bilingual," which recognizes that the students will not be giving up their home language but, instead, adding English as a second (or subsequent) language and that their home language is an asset to be built upon. This is considered an "additive" approach to multilingualism (Lambert, Mallea, & Young, 1975).

In contrast to subtractive English-only instruction, dual-language immersion has emerged over the past thirty years as the program of choice to prepare students for the global, multilingual, and multicultural world that they will be entering as adults. In a dual-language immersion program, instruction is provided in English and a partner language, with a minimum of 10% of the day taught in English and a minimum of 50% of the day taught in the partner language. The most common dual-language immersion program models start no later than kindergarten, and in a 90:10 program, sequential literacy is taught, first focusing on developing literacy in the partner language and then adding literacy in English.

In a 50:50 dual-language immersion program, the instructional time is split equally between English and the partner language, and literacy in each language is developed simultaneously. It is considered an additive program because all students add an additional language to their linguistic repertoire, becoming not just bilingual but biliterate, attaining high levels of biliteracy in English as well as the program's partner language. In addition, the cognitive benefits of a dual-language program are demonstrated by the typical pattern of students in dual-language immersion programs achieving at higher levels academically than their peers who are not participating in a dual-language immersion program (Collier & Thomas, 2017; Thomas & Collier, 2002).

Dual-language immersion programs consider the students' home languages and cultures as assets to build upon. Instruction is intellectually challenging, integrating and scaffolding content learning, literacy, and language development and appropriate for the students' grade level and level of language proficiency, giving the students full access to standards-based instruction and curriculum. Strong family and community partnerships are also hallmarks of a dual-language immersion program.

Dual-language immersion programs are an outstanding example of an additive approach to multilingualism that prepares students who are native speakers of English and those who are not for the global, multilingual, and multicultural world that awaits them as adults.

Appendix C

Spanish Book Collections to Inspire Joy and Engagement

Heather Robertson-Devine

One of the most important tools for literacy instruction is books. A story or information provokes curiosity, wonder, and reflection beyond oneself. However, the message to classroom teachers is often that test scores are more important than joy and engagement. I want students to experience the joy and excitement of books. As a child, I was surrounded by many books that were read to me and that I would get lost in for hours.

When it was independent reading time in my classroom, I wanted students to experience the love of reading. Unfortunately, my classroom was lacking a critical mass of high-quality Spanish books. For years, many studies have linked the number of books in a school to standardized test achievement, cognitive ability, and reading comprehension test scores (Mulligan & Landrigan, 2018). Books are a critical resource to increase student achievement.

Over the past 12 years I have been developing Spanish book collections, using my experience as a teacher and coach in a bilingual program that transitioned to a two-way dual-language program. My goal was to create collections that were equitable to English collections, yet diverse and comprehensive for our bilingual and dual-language classrooms. To achieve my goal, I applied the following principles to curate Spanish book collections that support equitable and comprehensive Spanish literacy instruction.

QUANTITY ALIGNS WITH LANGUAGE ALLOCATION

An equitable book collection demands a critical mass of books. There are many opinions on the optimal number of books needed to impact academic achievement. In *It's All About the Books*, Mulligan and Landrigan (2018) compile opinions from literacy experts.

- Fountas and Pinnell's research suggests that teachers need between 300 and 600 titles in their classroom library.
- The International Reading Association recommends that schools need to have at least seven books per student.
- The American Library Association suggests 300 titles in a classroom library with supplements from a well-stocked school library.
- Lucy Calkins wrote, "a general rule of thumb when provisioning for libraries is about 30 books per child as a starting point."
- Kelly Gallagher, author of *Readicide*, suggests that nothing less than a classroom book flood will suffice—"not 200 titles but *2,000.*"

These suggested numbers do not consider language of instruction; therefore, dual-language programs must account for the language allocation. Language allocation as defined by Beeman and Urow: "Using instructional minutes allocated for the day or week (do not include specials or lunch/recess), determine how much instructional time students spend in Spanish and how much of their instructional time is in English" (2013). The book collections should reflect such language allocation. Further, if a school has a combination of bilingual and monolingual classrooms, then it is important to consider the ratio of the students in each. The percentage of the day instructing in Spanish should equal the percentage of Spanish books in the school. For example, if the entire school followed the language allocation of 80% Spanish, 20% English, then 60% of the books should be in Spanish.

However, it is important to consider the whole school population. For example, if half of the school population is monolingual and the other half dual language, then the ratio of materials should reflect the ratio of the student population and their language allocation.

QUALITY

It is not only important to have enough books to meet the student population and their languages, but it is also important that the books are of high quality. Considerations for quality include the age and durability of the books.

Commonly, books older than eleven years old are considered "outdated." Content and relevance of topics tend to change over time. Further, a library book if well circulated will last three to five years. If a book is still around after ten years, it probably isn't circulating, so it's time to remove it and make room for books that will circulate.

PSYCHOSOCIAL USES FOR LITERATURE

Books del Sur categorizes books in three categories:

1. books originally written in a language other than Spanish,
2. books written in both English and Spanish or bilingual books, and
3. books written in Spanish.

Each type of book reflects the culture and norms of the author and publisher. Students are then able to see themselves in these different types of texts because dual-language students identify in many different ways. For example, some dual-language students are from monolingual English U.S. homes, and they are much more likely to identify with books that are translated.

This is what Rudine Sims Bishop has termed windows, mirrors, and sliding glass doors (1990). Books that provide characters and events with which readers can identify and through which they can consider their own actions, beliefs, and emotions are books that *mirror* a child's life and experiences. This enhances their connection to the book and, therefore, increases their engagement and comprehension. Some books provide *windows*. They introduce readers to what the world may look like through others' eyes and offer a chance to further construct their own views of self and the world. These different perspectives in books are essential because, "When children cannot find themselves reflected in the books they read, or when the images they see are distorted, negative, or laughable, they learn a powerful lesson about how they are devalued in the society of which they are a part. Our classrooms need to be places where all children from all the cultures that make up the salad bowl of American society can find their mirrors" (Billings et al., 2017).

ORGANIZATION

Book collections should also reflect the different genres of texts, themes, and levels. Books organized by themes allow readers to select texts based on their interest. Books organized by genre help students to see patterns in texts that further their comprehension. Books organized by levels ensure that the books are within a student's zone of proximal development (ZPD). The ZPD is defined as the space between what a learner can do without assistance and what a learner can do with adult guidance or in collaboration with more capable peers (Billings et al., 2017). Therefore, the organization of books by level further supports the students' independent reading. Organizing a book collection in a variety of ways supports readers selecting books that they will engage with at that moment.

ACCESSIBILITY

Who uses books, how books are used, and where they are available are key factors for accessibility. Some books are used for teacher-centered instruction through whole-group read-alouds. They expose students to grade level or above texts with the objective of increasing vocabulary and linguistic structures to further their internal linguistic repertoire. These books are often stored away from student general access but are critical for holistic literacy development.

Some books are published for small-group instruction in specific literacy skills to enhance comprehension of texts within the students ZPD. These texts scaffold instruction to increase students' independent reading ability. These books are limited in student accessibility and managed by a teacher; therefore, they are often found in book rooms or stored around a kidney table where the instruction takes place.

Books that support independent student reading are found in a classroom or school library. These books should be physically accessible and organized in a variety of ways so that students can select them based on their purpose in reading as described in evaluation criteria 4.

IT'S MORE THAN BOOKS

The abundance of books and books that meet the above-mentioned principles are the foundation of student biliteracy. However, educating a biliterate student requires more than books. It requires social, dynamic, responsive instruction that is given in a caring, supportive environment. Our desire is to inspire and support teachers and educators with books that come alive in students' hearts and minds.

Appendix D

The Power of a Paired Curricular Framework

Amy Mosquera

Cross-language connections. Metalanguage. Bridging. Translanguaging. What do all of these terms have in common? Connections. Our emerging bilingual students need teachers to bring the two languages together to make connections; one way to accomplish this is for dual-language programs to develop a paired curricular framework as a roadmap for facilitating these connections. The bilingual brain cannot wait for us to bring the two languages together at a later time, so what should educators do? Work collaboratively to develop a year-long, content-integrated, paired-curriculum map.

You might be thinking, *Our district has a scope and sequence that all teachers follow, in any program*. By expecting our dual-language teachers to follow a monolingual scope and sequence as well as its pacing, frustration can ensue. In dual-language programming, the goals are different from a general-education, monolingual classroom. The goals for all dual-language programs are bilingualism and biliteracy, grade-level academic achievement in two languages, and sociocultural competence (Guiding Principles for Dual Language Education, CAL, 2018). If the goals are different, the scope and sequence look different to allow for the development of two languages. In an effort to align the two programs, districts can create a year-long map that aligns their themes and standards; however, some standards as well as the pacing will look different.

Best practice in a dual-language program is to develop content-integrated units that are standards based while maintaining equal status of both languages. This year-long map identifies what should be taught and in what language and is adaptable to meet the needs of the multilingual learners we serve. As teams are developing these maps, pay special attention not only to the content standards but also the literacy standards to enhance biliteracy development.

If our goal is truly biliteracy, then we need to ensure that the literacy standards are evident and paired or coordinated in the map. Coordinating and connecting the language and literacy environments will naturally help students to make connections in their learning. Teachers can capitalize on these connections to deepen students' metalinguistic awareness. The goal when developing this paired curricular framework is to create a seamless and connected learning experience for our multilingual students that meets the three goals of dual-language education.

The first step in developing this curricular framework is to creating a standards-based sequence for language and literacy development in both languages. This scope and sequence should provide the roadmap for what standards teachers will teach and in each language. This map, separated into themes and big ideas, should include literacy and content standards plus state proficiency standards. Districts must ensure that Spanish language arts standards are included in the map. Many states have adopted Spanish language arts standards or follow the San Diego Common Core en español standards (www.commoncore-espanol.sdcoe.net). If a framework/scope and sequence are not provided or don't reflect the program, teachers will not have a clear vision of how to make connections for their students, running the risk of teaching subjects in isolation and out of context.

The demographics in our school districts are changing. Many of our students are coming in as simultaneous bilinguals and should be instructed as such. It's important to provide instruction that is connected between languages and allows for students to use their entire linguistic repertoire. Paired literacy has been researched as an effective way to enhance biliteracy instruction with emerging bilingual students. The paired literacy approach is an essential component of the Literacy Squared biliteracy model (Soltero-Gonzales, Sparrow, Butvilofsky, Escamilla, & Hopewell, 2014).

In this approach, students are taught reading and writing in two languages simultaneously beginning in kindergarten. Literacy instruction in the second language is not delayed until the student has literacy skills in one language and fosters the connection for students in literacy while exposing them to a variety of genres. When dual-language programs develop content-integrated biliteracy units without paying special attention to the literacy standards, they run the risk of these units being so content driven that literacy is not taught explicitly. In a strong curricular framework, the content and the language are mapped out coupled with the literacy standards and paired between language environments.

It is suggested that these year-long maps designate one language to do the heavy cognitive lifting by integrating content and literacy while the second language supports and connects to the other language without duplicating or translating. Many times, in a dual-language program, each language is not only trying to fit in literacy but also a content-integrated unit according to the district's content allocation. This approach relies heavily on content teaching in a short amount of time, which causes teachers to teach at the surface level without having the time to dig deeper into the learning and stretch students.

When teachers feel rushed for time and feel the need to "cover" everything, they run the risk of leaving student learning behind. These maps should put students in charge of their learning, engaging them in applicable tasks that provide opportunities for inquiry, having students wonder and question while developing a passion for social justice.

In a paired literacy and paired language environment, typically in kindergarten through second grade the heavy cognitive lifting is done in the target language. Many districts have also chosen to alternate which language will do the heavy lifting of both content and literacy starting in second or third grade. Using the district's content and language allocation, they map out their themes and decide which language will do the heavy lifting. Once that has been decided, the pairing begins. As teams of teachers look at the theme, big ideas, and essential questions of their units, they look for ways to make connections to the theme in the second language. It is possible to make connections across language environments in many ways.

One way is to pair informational text with literature text. For example, if the heavy lifting is being taught in English and is focusing on the content area of social studies with the theme of community, teams can connect and support that theme in Spanish by focusing on identity and how the students fit into their community. Teams then can select informational texts paired with literature texts in English. In addition, quality mentor texts need to be selected in Spanish to highlight a student's identity.

One fourth-grade team was especially creative in pairing the science unit theme, dangerous weather. The English teacher did the heavy cognitive lifting developing the content. Informational, content-focused texts were used in English while her teaching counterpart focused on myths and legends. You might wonder what the connection is between those two themes. The team found beautiful authentic myths and legends from a variety of Latin American countries written in Spanish. They chose myths and legends that focused on weather to use with their whole-group instruction. Students' end performance task was to create an informational slide show in English on how to stay safe during dangerous weather.

In Spanish, students collaboratively wrote a myth incorporating a weather phenomenon. The teacher did not have to reteach the content information in Spanish because students were automatically able to transfer what they learned in English into their myths in Spanish. This type of connection could not have been possible without the strong paired curriculum map. This curriculum map also helped this team of teachers with planning and collaboration. They planned together every week to ensure that they were pairing standards and concepts. Students were able to see the connection between what they were learning in one language to the other.

Developing these maps and biliteracy units takes time and commitment from administrators and teachers. Time and resources must be allocated to planning this curricular framework to ensure not only that connections are being made across languages, but that an equitable amount of quality resources is dedicated to each language.

Cognitive Heavy Lifting

- Science Unit: Living and Nonliving Things
- Science Unit: Earth's Changes
- Social Studies: Roles and Responsibilities in our Community
- Social Studies: Economy and Financial Literacy

Partner Language

- Fables and Fairy Tales
- How I've Changed Over Time
- My Home Community
- Personal Experience: Saving Money and Working toward a Goal

One important step when developing these year-long maps is not only to assure that you are covering your state standards, but that you are collecting quality mentor texts for teachers to use when developing units and teaching. If we skip this step in gathering quality mentor texts in both languages, teachers are left trying to find resources on their own time or simply translate materials from English to the target language. This results in added extra work for teachers, and it runs the risk of teaching the material not as rigorously, and/or not exposing students to grade-level mentor text.

In conclusion, strong paired-curriculum maps that reflect the goals of a dual-language program result in improved student learning and collaboration between teachers. The road is clear in supporting teachers to know what they are to teach in each language, which helps to facilitate connections between language and literacy environments.

Appendix E

Acentos ortográficos en español: *A Simple Guide*

Dr. Kimberley D. Kennedy

La mayoría de las palabras en español NO llevan acentos ortográficos (o tildes). Vamos a repasar alguna información para determinar si una palabra lleva acento ortográfico o no.

1. Las palabras multisilábicas

Most multisyllabic words (those with two or more syllables) in Spanish do *not* have accent marks. In the case of multisyllabic words, it's directly tied to spoken Spanish. So, to understand this section more fully, make sure you say sample Spanish words aloud in an exaggerated way when determining where the stressed (or strong) syllable is.

a. Why are most words in Spanish written without an accent mark?

Because Spanish has only two natural pronunciation patterns. That's it. And thankfully, most words are pronounced in an expected way using one of the natural pronunciation patterns. We will call those words *palabras conformistas* because they conform to one of the two expected pronunciation patterns.

When a word does not follow one of the two natural pronunciation patterns, it will carry an accent mark to signal that it breaks away from one of the expected pronunciation patterns. We will call these words *palabras rebeldes*, because they rebel against what is expected.

b. What are the two natural pronunciation patterns?

Natural pronunciation pattern #1: The first natural pronunciation pattern in Spanish encompasses words ending in a *vowel, -n, or -s*. If a word ends in a vowel, -n, or -s, the stressed syllable naturally falls on the *second-to-last* syllable. In other words:

- palabras terminando en una vocal, -n, o -s = la sílaba fuerte es la penúltima

Examples of *palabras conformistas* for this pattern include *gato, baño, botella, caminamos, libro, ventana,* and *escriben*. Because they conform to the natural pronunciation pattern (i.e., pronounced as expected), they will *not* typically carry an accent mark.

What happens to a word that ends in a vowel, -n, or -s where the stressed syllable is *not* the second-to-last one? Then, it's considered a *palabra rebelde* and will have an accent mark over the stressed syllable. Words such as *teléfono, jardín, balón, comí,* and *sílabas* have written accent marks over the stressed syllable.

Natural pronunciation pattern #2: The second natural pronunciation pattern in Spanish encompasses words ending in a *consonant besides -n or -s*. If a word ends in a consonant besides -n or -s, the stressed syllable naturally falls on the *last* syllable. In other words:

- palabras terminando en una consonante menos -n, o -s = la sílaba fuerte es la última

Examples of *palabras conformistas* for this pattern include *hablar, tomar, animal,* and *nariz*. Because they conform to the natural pronunciation pattern (i.e., pronounced as expected), they will *not* typically carry an accent mark.

What happens to a word that ends in a consonant besides -n or -s where the stressed syllable is *not* the last one? Then, it's considered a *palabra rebelde* and will have an accent mark over the stressed syllable. Words such as *difícil, lápiz,* and *árbol* have written accent marks over the stressed syllable.

c. El diagrama de flujo

Gee! That's a lot to remember, right? Well, based on my research (Kennedy, 2010, 2011), I developed a simple flowchart so that you and your students may determine quickly (and eventually automatically) whether a multisyllabic word carries an accent mark. All you have to do is ask yourself two questions about the word. Here are the steps to the flowchart:

- Ask yourself question #1 (in the top tier): The first question is in the top box of the flowchart and has you pay attention to the last letter of the word: "*La palabra termina en una vocal, -n, o -s?*"
- Follow the arrows based on how you answer question #1: "*Sí*" or "*No.*"
- Ask yourself question #2 (in the middle tier): The second question has you pay attention to where the stressed syllable is. If the word ends in a vowel, -n, or -s, the question is: *¿la sílaba fuerte es la penúltima?* If the word ends in a consonant besides -n or -s, the question is: *¿la sílaba fuerte es la última?*
- Follow the arrows based on how you answer question #2: "*Sí*" or "*No.*"
- Follow the instructions in the bottom-tier boxes. If you answer "*Sí*" to the second question, the word is a *palabra conformista* and will not have an accent mark. And you guessed it! If you answer "*No*" to the second question, the word is a *palabra rebelde* and will, indeed, have an accent mark over the stressed syllable.

Practice using the flowchart when you write. The goal is to start internalizing the two natural pronunciation patterns (the two sides of the flowchart) and whether a word is "*conformista*" or "*rebelde.*" The more you use it, the more automatic it will become.

2. Las vocales vecinas (Kennedy, 2021)

Besides multisyllabic words (previous section), adjacent vowels and how they behave are important to understand so you can determine whether an accent mark is needed and if so, where it should be placed.

a. Las vocales

¿Cómo se portan las vocales vecinas? Let's focus on the natural pronunciation and behavior of Spanish vowels.

There are two types of vowels and their corresponding phonemes:

- *abierta tónica* = "Hangry": a, e, o
- *cerrada átona* = *Satisfecha*: i, u

These types will make sense if you place the back of your hand lightly under your chin and say each vowel sound. Notice what your mouth does.

Vocales abiertas. Did your mouth open wide to produce the sounds for a, e, and o? *Con razón que se llaman vocales abiertas, ¿verdad?* I half-jokingly call these three vowels the "hangry" vowels (you know—a combination of hungry and angry), because they don't—or better yet, can't—share the same syllable. For a syllable to be formed, it must contain a vowel sound (or sounds), and you must open your mouth for each individual syllable. Because you must open your mouth to produce each *vocal abierta*, each one would automatically claim its own syllable. In other words, they won't share their "*papa*" or "*comida*" with another *vocal abierta*, which is why I refer to them as "hangry."

Vocales cerradas. What did your mouth do to produce the sounds for i and u? I bet your jaw barely opens, right? It makes sense, then, that i and u are *vocales cerradas.* It's tied directly to Spanish-language oracy and pronunciation. Because you don't have to open your mouth as wide to make the two *vocales cerradas,* I refer to them as *vocales satisfechas,* because they can share syllables with other vowels. In other words, they can be next to other vowels without needing or claiming their own syllable. Keep in mind these traits of the *vocales* as we get into the different categories of *vocales vecinas.*

b. Categorías de vocales vecinas

Diptongos. *Un diptongo es la unión de dos vocales dentro de la misma sílaba.* Diphthongs can be formed by the following vowel combinations (with examples provided):

- *abierta + cerrada:* aire, peine, jaula, aplaudir
- cerrada + abierta: cielo, copiar, tierra, tuvieras
- cerrada + cerrada: fui, viuda, ruido

Triptongos. *Un triptongo es la unión de tres vocales dentro de la misma sílaba.* A triphthong can only be formed by an open vowel (a, e, o) between two closed vowels (i, u). The letter "y" takes the place of the "i" phoneme in some spellings of words, as you can see in the examples below:
cerrada + abierta + cerrada: miau, Uruguay, Paraguay, guau, buey
Hiatos. *Un hiato se forma cuando hay dos vocales vecinas que se separan en sílabas distintas. Hiatos* are formed in one of two ways:

- when two *vocales abiertas* (a, e, o) are next to each other. (Remember "hangry" vowels need their own syllable; they will never share a syllable even though they are next to one another.)

- when an accent mark is placed on a *vocal cerrada* (i, e). (This is where accent marks come into play, because a *vocal cerrada* stops being *satisfecha* and becomes "hangry" when it has an accent mark. *Cuando la vocal cerrada lleva un acento ortográfico, quiere su propia papita o comidita ya.*)

Therefore, a hiatus can be formed by the following combinations (with some examples provided):

- *abierta + abierta* (two "hangry" vowels): creer, crear, croar, video
- *abierta + cerrada (la cerrada se pone "hangry" con el acento ortográfico)*: Raúl, oído, raíz, sonreímos
- *cerrada + abierta (la cerrada se pone "hangry" con el acento ortográfico)*: día, María, mío, continúa

c. ¿Dónde se pone el acento ortográfico cuando hay vocales vecinas?

Hiatos con vocales cerradas. As mentioned above, "*los hiatos*" with closed vowels need an accent mark over the closed vowel so it can have its own syllable as in the word *mío*.

Palabras rebeldes con vocales vecinas. This part can be a little tricky, because we are combining what you learned from section 1 (*las palabras multisilábicas*) and this section (*las vocales vecinas*). *Cuando las vocales quieren seguir juntas en la misma sílaba (o sea, seguir como diptongos o triptongos) pero la palabra no sigue la pronunciación natural, vas a poner el acento ortográfico en la vocal abierta.* Why do you put the accent over the open vowel? Well, because it's already hangry so you're not changing the nature of it. However, if you were to put the accent mark over a closed vowel, you'd change its nature, making it hangry, and it wouldn't be able to stay in that diphthong or triphthong as intended. Let's look at some examples. The following words contain diphthongs composed of an open and a closed vowel. Because they are *palabras rebeldes*, they need an accent mark over the open vowel (not over the closed vowel):

- desp<u>ué</u>s
- b<u>éi</u>sbol
- cop<u>ió</u>
- tamb<u>ié</u>n
- rec<u>ié</u>n
- h<u>ué</u>rfano
- murc<u>ié</u>lago
- agres<u>ió</u>n

Now you know why the words ending in -ion in Spanish have an accent over the "o" like in *calificación, comprensión, integración,* and *presentación.* They are *palabras rebeldes* with a diphthong. That's why you put the accent mark over the "o" (not the "i").

3. Los homónimos

Have you ever noticed that sometimes "*te*" has an accent mark and sometimes not (among other seemingly similar words)? Spanish differentiates between certain homonyms (words that sound the same but have different meanings) by placing an accent over one and not the other.

One way to remember which one carries the accent mark is that the word with more grammatical weight or importance usually has the *acento ortográfico.* For example, the noun for tea is more important grammatically in a sentence than a personal pronoun, right? Therefore, "*té*" meaning what you drink carries an accent mark whereas "*te*" meaning the direct or indirect pronoun for "you" does not. This and other examples can be found in the following table:

Table E.1

Palabras con la tilde	Palabras sin la tilde
tú *(pronombre personal)* **Tú** *vives aquí, ¿verdad?*	tu *(adjetivo posesivo)* **Tu** *perro ladra mucho.*
mí *(pronombre personal)* A **mí** *me gusta nadar.*	mi *(adjetivo posesivo)* **Mi** *gato tiene rayas.*
él *(pronombre personal)* **Él** *va a la fiesta.*	el *(artículo)* **El** *sol salió por la tarde.*
té *(sustantivo; = bebida/infusión)* *Tomamos* **té.**	te *(pronombre personal)* *¿* **Te** *gusta la pizza?*
sé *(de los verbos ser o saber)* Yo **sé** *mucho del tema.*	se *(pronombre reflexivo)* **Se** *baña en la noche.*
más *(adverbio de cantidad)* Me regalaron *tres libros* **más.**	mas *(conjunción; = pero)* Huele rico, **mas** *ya comí.*
dé *(del verbo dar)* Cuando me **dé** *las noticias, estaría muy contenta.*	de *(preposición)* Es la casa **de** *mi amiga.*
sí *(afirmativo)* **Sí,** *voy a ir.*	si *(conjunción condicional)* **Si** *pones un abrigo, vas a estar más cómdo.*
sólo *(adverbio; = solamente)* **Sólo** *me quedan 2 lápices.*	solo *(adjetivo masculino)* Miguel está **solo** *en su casa.*
aún* *(adverbio; = todavía)* **Aún** *no llega.*	aun* *(adverbio; = incluso/ hasta/ también/ ni siquiera)* **Aun** *los maestros necesitan descansar de vez en cuando.*

Todas las palabras en la tabla de arriba son homónimos excepto "aun" y "aún." Las palabras "aún" y "aun" no son homónimos, porque "aún" tiene dos sílabas y "aun" sólo una. I put them in this section because they fit here better than anywhere else.

4. Las palabras interrogativas y exclamativas

Common interrogative and exclamatory words in Spanish carry accent marks. Don't ask me *por qué.* See what I did there? That's why most interrogative words and exclamatory words will carry an accent mark even though they are officially *palabras conformistas* and follow the expected natural pronunciation pattern that we covered in the first section.

a. Palabras interrogativas y exclamativas directas

The following table includes these words along with examples.

Table E.2

Palabra	Como palabras interrogativas y exclamativas directas
quién / quiénes	¿Con quién te vas?
qué	¿Por qué te fuiste?
	¿Qué te dijo ayer?
	¡Qué bárbaro!
dónde / adónde	¿De dónde vienen?
cuánto / cuánta / cuántos / cuántas	¿Cuánto cuesta?
cuán	¡Cuán peludo es tu perro!
cuándo	¿Hasta cuándo se quedan?
cuál / cuáles	¿Cuál vas a escoger?
cómo	¿Cómo se llama?
	¡Cómo me he divertido!

b. Palabras interrogativas o exclamativas indirectas

That's pretty straight forward, right? Here's where it gets a little trickier. Interrogative and exclamatory words used *indirectly* within sentences also need accent marks. *La siguiente oración, por ejemplo, tiene tres ejemplos de palabras interrogativas indirectas: No sé por **qué** se fue, con **quién** está, o por **dónde** anda.*

They don't need an accent mark when they're used as conjunctions, adverbs, or pronouns within sentences, such as: *Me dijo **que** me iba a regalar algo. Ella fue **quien** me regaló la taza. Te lo va a dar **cuando** llegues.*

Figure E.1. Diagrama de Flujo: A ver si una palabra multisilabica necesita un acento ortografico. Created by **Kimberley D. Kennedy**

c. Palabras interrogativas o exclamativas como sustantivos

These words also need accent marks when they are used as nouns, as in the following sentence: *En la enseñanza, es importante explicar el por **qué** y el **cómo** de cada lección.*

References

Alfaro, C. (2022, January 7). *Code switching takes a lot of skill and a complex command of grammar.* Retrieved from https://www.sandiegouniontribune.com/opinion/commentary/story/2022-01-07/opinion-code-switching-takes-a-lot-of-skill-and-a-complex-command-of-grammar.

Álvarez-Cañizo, M., Cueva, E., Cuetos, F., & Suárez-Coalla, P. (2020). Reading fluency and reading comprehension in Spanish secondary students. *Psicothema, 32*(1), 75–83. https://doi.org/10.7334/psicothema2019.196.

American Library Association. (2010). *Position statement on the value of independent reading in the school library program.* Retrieved from http://www.ala.org/aasl/advocacy/resources/statements/ind-reading.

American Reading Company. (n.d.). *Correlation with other leveling systems.* https://www.americanreading.com/documents/Correlations-With-Other-Leveling-Systems-Spanish.pdf.

Beeman, K., & Urow, C. (2013). *Teaching for biliteracy: Strengthening bridges between languages.* Philadelphia, PA: Caslon.

Bialystok, E. (2011). Reshaping the mind: The benefits of bilingualism. *Canadian Journal of Experimental Psychology (Revue canadienne de psychologie experimentale), 65*(4), 229–35. https://doi.org/10.1037/a0025406.

Biemiller, A. (2003, Spring). Oral comprehension sets the ceiling on reading comprehension. *American Educator* [Electronic edition]. Retrieved from https://www.aft.org/periodical/american-educator/spring-2003/oral-comprehension-sets-ceiling-reading.

Billings, Elsa, & Aida Walqui. (2017). *Zone of proximal development: an affirmative perspective in teaching ELLs.* New York State Education Department.

Bloome, D., Power, C. S., Morton, C. B., Otto, S., & Shuart-Paris, N. (2005). *Discourse analysis and the study of classroom language and literacy events: A microethnographic perspective.* Mahwah, NJ: Lawrence Erlbaum.

Britton, J. (1983). Writing and the story of the world. In B. Kroll & E. Wells (Eds.), *Explorations in the development of writing theory, research, and practice* (pp. 3–30). New York: Wiley.

Center for Applied Linguistics. (2016). *What literacy skills transfer across English and Spanish and which need to be taught explicitly in each language? Two-Way Immersion.* https://www.cal.org/twi/toolkit/QA/lit_a3.htm.

Civil, M. (2017). Preface. In S. Celedón-Pattichis, D. Y. White, & M. Civil (Eds.), *Access and equity: Promoting high-quality mathematics in pre-K–grade 2* (pp. v–viii). National Council of Teachers of Mathematics.

Collier, Virginia, & Thomas, Wayne. (2017). Validating the power of bilingual schooling: thirty-two years of large-scale, longitudinal research. *Annual Review of Applied Linguistics, 37,* 203–17.

Colon, I. T. (2019). Interview: Dr. Sonia Soltero on the importance of cross-linguistic connections and metabilingual awareness. *New America.* https://www.newamerica .org/education-policy/edcentral/interview-dr-sonia-soltero-importance-cross -linguistic-connections-and-metabilingual-awareness/.

Cummins, J. (2007). Rethinking monolingual instructional strategies in multilingual classrooms. *Canadian Journal of Applied Linguistics, 10,* 221–40.

de Manrique, A. M. B., & Signorini, A. (1994). Phonological awareness, spelling and reading abilities in Spanish-speaking children. *British Journal of Educational Psychology, 64*(3), 429–39. https://doi.org/10.1111/j.2044-8279.1994.tb01114.x.

Defior, Sylvia, Jiménez Fernández, Gracia, & Serrano, Francisca. (2006). Spelling acquisition: A transversal study of Spanish children. *International Journal of Learning: Annual Review, 12*(10), 293–300. doi: 10.18848/1447-9494/CGP/ v12i10/48218.

Delpit, L. (2006). *Other people's children: Cultural conflict in the classroom.* New York: New Press.

Dove, M., Honigsfeld, A., & Cohan, A. (2014). *Beyond core expectations.* Thousand Oaks, CA: Corwin.

Dixson, A. D., & Fasching-Varner, K. J. (2009). This is how we do it: Helping teachers understand culturally relevant pedagogy in diverse classrooms. In C. Compton-Lilly (Ed.), *Breaking the silence: Recognizing the social and cultural resources students bring to the classroom.* Newark, DE: International Reading Association.

Duke, N. K., & Mesmer, H. A. E. (2019). Phonics faux pas: Avoiding instructional missteps in teaching letter-sound relationships. *American Educator, 42*(4), 12–16. Win 2018–2019 ERIC Number: EJ1200223 ISSN: ISSN-0148–432X. https://files .eric.ed.gov/fulltext/EJ1200223.pdf.

Dyson, A. H. (2008). Staying in the (curricular) lines: Practice constraints and possibilities in childhood writing. *Written Communication, 25*(1), 119–59.

Eeds, M., & Wells, D. (1989). Grand conversations: An exploration of meaning construction in literature study groups. *Research in the Teaching of English, 23*(1), 4–29.

Eliason, C., & Jenkins, L. (2012). *A practical guide to early childhood curriculum* (9th ed.). Boston, MA: Pearson Education.

Equity Literacy Institute. (2021). *About equity literacy.* Retrieved from https://www .equityliteracy.org/equity-literacy.

Escamilla, K. (2001). Bilingual means two: Assessment issues, early literacy and Spanish speaking children. In *Reading research symposium for second language learners* (pp. 1–16). Washington, DC: National Clearinghouse for Bilingual Education.

Fisher, D., & Frey, N. (2008). *Better learning through structured teaching: A framework for the gradual release of responsibility* (p. 4). Alexandria, VA: ASCD.

Ford, K., & Palacios, R. (2015). *Early literacy instruction in Spanish: Teaching the beginning reader.* ¡Colorín colorado! https://www.colorincolorado.org/article/early -literacy-instruction-spanish-teaching-beginning-reader.

Fountas, I. C., & Pinnell, G. S. (1996). *Guided reading: Good first teaching for all children* (1st ed.). Portsmouth, NH: Heineman.

Fountas, I. C., & Pinnell, G. S. (2012). *F&P text level gradient.* https://www .fountasandpinnell.com/textlevelgradient/.

Fountas, I. C., & Pinnell, G. S. (2017). *Guided reading* (2nd ed.). Portsmouth, NH: Heineman.

Fountas, I. C., & Pinnell, G. S. (2019). Level books, not children: The role of text levels in literacy instruction. Retrieved from https://www.fountasandpinnell.com/ shared/resources/FPL_LevelBooksNotKids_Whitepaper.pdf.

García, O. (2009). Education, multilingualism and translanguaging in the 21st century. In Ajit Mohanty, Minati Panda, Robert Phillipson, & Tove Skutnabb-Kangas (Eds.), *Multilingual education for social justice: Globalising the local* (pp. 128– 45). New Delhi: Orient Blackswan (formerly Orient Longman).

García, O., Johnson, S. I., & Seltzer, K. (2017). The translanguaging classroom: Leveraging student bilingualism for learning. *Journal of immersion and Content-Based Language-Education.* doi: 10.1080/09500782.2016.1255224.

Gay, G. (2018). *Culturally responsive teaching: Theory, research, and practice.* New York: Teachers College Press.

Gay, G. (2002). Preparing for culturally responsive teaching. *Journal of Teacher Education, 53*(2): 106–16. https://www.cwu.edu/teaching-learning/sites/cts.cwu .edu.teaching-learning/files/documents/PreparingforCulturallyResponsiveTeach ing,%20Geneva%20Gay.pdf.

Grosjean, F. (1989). Neurolinguists, beware! The bilingual is not two monolinguals in one person. *Brain and Language, 36*(1), 3–15.

Grosjean, F. (2010). *Bilingual: Life and reality.* Cambridge, MA: Harvard University Press.

Grosjean, F. (2016). What is translanguaging: An interview with Ofelia Garcia. Retrieved October 6, 2019, from https://www.psychologytoday.com/us/blog/life -bilingual/201603/what-is-translanguaging.

Guilamo, A. (2021). The science of reading in dual language. *Language magazine.* Retrieved November 10, 2021, from https://www.languagemagazine.com/2021/04 /20/the-science-of-reading-in-dual-language/.

Hanselman, P., Bruch, S. K., Gamoran, A., & Borman, G. D. (2014). Threat in context: School moderation of the impact of social identity threat on racial/ethnic achievement gaps. *Sociology of Education, 87*(2), 106–24.

Harris, V. J. (Ed.). (1997). *Using multiethnic literature in the K–8 classroom.* Norwood, MA: Christopher-Gordon.

Illinois School Board of Education. (2013). *Illinois early learning and development standards: For preschool.* Retrieved from https://www.isbe.net/Documents/early _learning_standards.pdf.

International Dyslexia Association. (2018). *Knowledge and practice standards for teachers of reading* (2nd ed.). Retrieved from https://dyslexiaida.org/knowledge -and-practices/.

Jennings, L. B., & Mills, H. (2009). Constructing a discourse of inquiry: Findings from a five-year ethnography at one elementary school. *Teachers College Record, 111*(7), 1583–618.

Johnston, P., Woodside-Jiron, H., & Day, J. (2000). *Teaching and learning literate epistemologies.* National Research Center on English Learning & Achievement. Report series 13009. Retrieved from http://cela.albancy.edu/epist/index.html.

Keene, E. (2006). Literacy learning presentation at Hinckley-Big Rock CUSD #429. August 16–17, 2006.

Ladson-Billings, G. (1994). *The dreamkeepers.* San Francisco, CA: Jossey-Bass.

Ladson-Billings G. (1995). Toward a theory of culturally relevant pedagogy. *American Educational Research Journal, 32*(3), 465–91. doi: 10.3102/00028312032003465.

Lambert, Wallace E., Mallea J., & Young, J. C. (1984). Culture and language as factors in learning and education. *Cultural Diversity and Canadian Education: Issues and Innovations, 130*, 233.

MacArthur, C., Graham, S., & Fitzgerald, J. (2016). *Handbook of writing research* (2nd ed.). New York: Guilford.

Marrero-Colon, M. (2021). *Translanguaging: Theory, concept, practice, stance . . . or all of the above?* Center for Applied Linguistics. https://www.cal.org/resource -center/publications-products/translanguaging.

McNair, J. C. (2010). Classic African American children's literature. *Reading Teacher, 64*(2), 96–105. doi: 10.1598/RT.64.2.2.

Mercer, N. (2008). The seeds of time: Why classroom dialogue needs a temporal analysis. *Journal of the Learning Sciences, 17*(1), 33–59.

MetaMetrics. (2021). *About Spanish lexile measures for reading.* https://lexile.com/ educators/understanding-lexile-measures/lexile-measures-spanish/.

Moats, L. C. (2020). *Teaching reading is rocket science.* Retrieved from https://www .aft.org/ae/summer2020/moats.

Moats, L. C., Glaser, D., & Tolman, C. (2016). *LETRS, Module 1: The challenge of learning to read book and training handouts* (2nd ed). Dallas, TX: Voyager Sopris Learning. http://cdn2.hubspot.net/hubfs/208815/2014-15_SchoolYear/LETRS /169261_Letrs2E_M1_29-38.pdf.

Moll, L. C., Amanti, C. Neff, D., & Gonzalez, N. (1992). Funds of knowledge for teaching: using a qualitative approach to connect homes and classrooms. In *Theory into Practice, 31*(2), 132–41.

Mulligan, T., & Landrigan, C. (2018). *It's all about the books: How to create bookrooms and classroom libraries that inspire readers.* Portsmouth, NH: Heinemann.

National Governors Association Center for Best Practices, Council of Chief State School Officers. (2010). *Appendix A: Research supporting key elements of the standards glossary of key terms. Common core state standards for English language arts.* Washington, DC.

National Governors Association Center for Best Practices, Council of Chief State School Officers. (2012). *California Spanish language development standards: Kindergarten through grade 12.* Washington, DC.

National Reading Panel (U.S.) & National Institute of Child Health and Human Development (U.S.). (2000). *Report of the National Reading Panel: Teaching children to read: an evidence-based assessment of the scientific research literature on reading and its implications for reading instruction.* U.S. Dept. of Health and Human Services, Public Health Service, National Institutes of Health, National Institute of Child Health and Human Development.

Nettles, D. H. (2006). *Comprehensive literacy instruction in today's classroom: The whole, the parts, and the heart.* Boston, MA: Allyn & Bacon.

Nieto, S., & Bode, P. (2013). *Affirming diversity: The sociopolitical context of multicultural education.* Upper Saddle River, NJ: Pearson.

Norman, K. (1992). *Thinking voices: The work of the national oracy project.* London: Hodder & Stoughton.

Nystrand, M. (2006). Research on the role of classroom discourse as it affects reading comprehension. *Research in the Teaching of English, 40*, 392–412.

Odlin, T. (1989). *Language transfer: Cross-linguistic influence in language learning* (Cambridge Applied Linguistics). Cambridge: Cambridge University Press. doi: 10.1017/CBO9781139524537.

Ordetx, K. (2021). What is the science of reading? *IMSE Journal.* Retrieved November 10, 2021, from https://journal.imse.com/what-is-the-science-of-reading/.

Palmer, P. J. (2017). *The courage to teach* (20th ed.). San Francisco, CA: Jossey-Bass.

Paris, D., & Alim, H. S. (2017). *Culturally sustaining pedagogies: Teaching and learning for justice in a changing world.* New York: Teachers College Press.

Pearson. (2018). *DRA2 and EDL2: Determining the reading grade level.* https://support.pearson.com/usclinical/s/article/DRA2-and-EDL2-Determining-the-Reading-Grade-Level

Potowski, Kim. (2010). Language diversity in the USA: Dispelling common myths and appreciating advantages. doi: 10.1017/CBO9780511779855.002.

Rasinski, T. V. (2003). *The fluent reader: Oral reading strategies for building word recognition, fluency, and comprehension.* London, UK: Scholastic Professional Books.

Richardson, J. (2016). *The next step forward in guided reading: An assess-decide-guide framework for supporting every reader.* New York: Scholastic.

Sánchez, M. T., García, O., & Solorza, C. (2018). Reframing language allocation policy in dual language bilingual education. *Bilingual Research Journal, 41*, 37–51.

Schwartz, A. I., Kroll, J. F., & Diaz, M. (2007). Reading words in Spanish and English: Mapping orthography to phonology in two languages. *Language and Cognitive Processes, 22*(1), 106–29.

Serravallo, J. (2018). *Understanding texts & readers: Responsive comprehension instruction with leveled texts.* Portsmouth, NH: Heinemann.

Sims Bishop, Rudine. (1990, Summer). Mirrors, windows, and sliding glass doors. *Perspectives: Choosing and Using Books for the Classroom, 6*(3).

Smith, David M. (2012). The American melting pot: A national myth in public and popular discourse. *National Identities, 14*(4), 387–402.

Soltero, S. W. (2016). *Dual language education: Program design and implementation.* Portsmouth, NH: Heinemann.

Temple, Charles A., Martinez, Miriam, Yokota, Junko, & Naylor, Alice. (1998). *Children's books in children's hands.* Boston, MA: Allyn and Bacon.

Texas Administrative Code. (2017). *Texas essential knowledge and skills for Spanish language arts and reading and English as a second language.* https://texreg.sos .state.tx.us/public/readtac$ext.ViewTAC?tac_view=5&ti=19&pt=2&ch=128&sch =A&rl=Y

Thomas, Wayne, & Collier, Virginia. (2002). *A national study of school effectiveness for language minority students' long-term academic achievement.* Santa Cruz, CA: Center for Research on Education, Diversity, and Excellence.

Turner, J. C. (1995). The influence of classroom contexts on young children's motivation for literacy. *Reading Research Quarterly, 30*(3), 410–41.

Turner, J., & Paris, S. G. (1995). How literacy tasks influence children's motivation for literacy. *Reading Teacher, 48*(8), 662–73.

Urow, C., Beeman, K., Warton, M, Karwoski, O., Nunez, P., & Hardt, D. (2019). Balanced literacy and biliteracy: How do writer's workshop and other balanced literacy routines fit into biliteracy instruction? *Soleado, 11*(3).

Valdés, G., Capitelli, S., & Alvarez, L. (2011). *Latino children learning English: Steps in the journey.* New York: Teachers College Press.

Wells, G., & Claxton, G. (Eds.). (2002). *Learning for life in the 21st century: Sociocultural perspectives on the future of education.* Retrieved from http://people .ucsc.edu/~gwe;;s/Files/Course_Folder/documents

Wilkinson, L. C., & Silliman, E. R. (2000). Classroom language and literacy learning. In M. L. Kamil, P. B. Mosenthal, P. D. Pearson, & R. Barr (Eds.), *Handbook of reading research* (Vol. 3, pp. 337–60). Mahwah, NJ: Lawrence Erlbaum.

Index

Page numbers in italics refer to figures and tables.

About the Authors and Contributors

Dr. Rocio del Castillo-Perez began her career as a school psychologist in Peru and has dedicated her professional career to being an advocate for educational equity and social justice. Her rich and diverse experience includes serving for more than 25 years in both public and private school systems, where she has received recognition and accolades for her work in the special education, bilingual, and dual-language settings. Rocio lives in northern Illinois with her husband, her two children, and two spoiled pit bulls. She currently serves as assistant superintendent for special services in Huntley Community School District 158 and as an adjunct professor at Northern Illinois University and St. Francis University.

Dr. Julia Stearns Cloat has spent the past twenty-five years working in public school districts in roles including elementary teacher, literacy specialist, instructional coach, and curriculum director. Julia is dedicated to providing equitable and accessible learning experiences through the development of curriculum and the continuous improvement of teachers. She lives in northern Illinois with her husband and her two children. She is passionate about the outdoors and spends every free moment hiking and camping. Julia currently works as the assistant superintendent of curriculum and instruction in Freeport School District 145 and as an adjunct professor at Northern Illinois University.

***

Geri Chaffee is president of PDO.org and a longtime education advocate. She is the host of *Por Nuestros Niños*, a national radio program and podcast that brings information and resources to Spanish-speaking parents and families so they can support their children's education journey. Most recently she founded Dreamers Academy, a dual-language immersion public charter school in Sarasota, Florida. Chaffee is a founding member of FABE, Florida's Association of Bilingual Education.

Douglas Fisher, PhD, is professor and chair of educational leadership at San Diego State University and a leader at Health Sciences High & Middle College, having been an early intervention teacher and elementary school educator. He is the recipient of an International Reading Association William S. Grey citation of merit, an exemplary leader award from the Conference on English Leadership of NCTE, as well as a Christa McAuliffe award for excellence in teacher education. He has published numerous articles on reading and literacy, differentiated instruction, and curriculum design as well as books such as *The Restorative Practices Playbook, PLC+: Better Decisions and Greater Impact by Design, Building Equity*, and *Better Learning Through Structured Teaching*. He can be reached at dfisher@mail.sdsu.edu.

Dr. Kimberley D. Kennedy, PhD, has been a bilingual educator (Spanish/ English) from PK–12 to university levels for more than twenty-five years. She has worked as a bilingual and special education teacher, as well as an instructional coach, literacy specialist, and university professor in the San Antonio and Austin, Texas, areas. Dr. Kennedy's work spans a deep understanding of multilingual learners' experiences in public education and addresses ways to differentiate instruction across the content areas for emergent bilingual learners. Dr. Kennedy has more than twenty publications in renowned journals and books. Currently, she supports future, new, and experienced bilingual, dual-language, and ESL educators and their programs through her company, Pocket Profe. Visit her at https://pocketprofe.com/ or contact her at info@ pocketprofe.com or on social media @pocketprofe.

Amy Mosquera is the CEO of Adelante Educational Specialists Group (www .adelantespecialists.com). She works closely with school districts, providing support and professional development in the areas of effective dual-language programming, second-language acquisition, and biliteracy instruction. With more than thirty years in education, her work has focused in the areas of second-language acquisition and bilingual education with an emphasis in dual-language/two-way immersion programming. Amy holds a master's degree in curriculum and instruction with an emphasis on bilingual education and a master's degree in educational leadership.

Dr. Kris Nicholls is CEO of Nicholls Educational Consulting (nichollseducationalconsulting.com) and has extensive experience in all areas of English learner and dual-language immersion education. Dr. Nicholls served as the Title III colead and dual immersion coordinator for Riverside County Office of Education and established its long-term English learner task force and Riverside County Seal of Multiliteracy program. She is the author of *From Subtractive to Additive: Transforming Your Transitional Bilingual Education Program to Dual Language Immersion* and *Fulfilling the Promise of Biliteracy: Creating a Successful and Sustainable Secondary Dual Language Program*. Dr. Nicholls can be reached at nichollseducationalconsulting@ gmail.com.

Heather Robertson-Devine, MEd, is the founder and owner of Books del Sur. She leads their mission to curate authentic Spanish literature from Latin America and Spain. She is driven by her seventeen years of dual-language teaching and coaching as a public-school educator in Wisconsin and California. She holds a master's degree in educational leadership and policy from California State University at Northridge and an undergraduate degree from the University of Wisconsin-Madison in international relations and Latin American and Iberian studies. She can be reached at heather@books-delsur.com.